# ROLE OF STRATEGIC MANAGEMENT IN BUSINESS ORGANIZATIONS

# Role of Strategic Management in Business Organizations

Copyright©: 2011-2018
Dr. W. A. Khan
ISBN: 9781791698447

Although the author has made every effort to verify the accuracy and completeness of the information contained in this book, but nevertheless, neither the author nor the publisher accepts responsibility for error or omission. This publication is not intended to render legal, or any other professional service. If legal advice or any other expert assistance is required, the services of a competent professional should be sought.

**CAUTION:** The readers are requested to respect this book as it contains orginal text of the Quran!

**Published by:**

**Dr. W. A. Khan**
**Uxbridge, London**
**First Edition – 2018**
**ISBN: 9781791698447**

# BOOKS IN SEARCH OF MANAGEMENT EXCELLENCE SERIES

1. TOWARDS UNDERSTANDING MANAGEMENT, MANAGEMENT PRINCIPLES AND PROCESS
2. **ROLE OF STRATEGIC MANAGEMENT IN BUSINESS ORGANIZATIONS**
3. MANAGERIAL ROLES, SKILLS AND COMPETENCIES IN BUSINESS ORGANIZATIONS
4. CREATIVE THINKING, PROBLEM SOLVING AND MANAGERIAL DECISION MAKING
5. ROLE OF DELEGATION IN MANAGEMENT EXCELLENCE OF BUSINESS ORGANIZATIONS
6. MANAGEMENT BY OBJECTIVES (MBO) IN ENTERPRISES
7. TIME AND SELF MANAGEMENT FOR EXECUTIVE EXCELLENCE
8. FUNDAMENTALS OF STRESS MANAGEMENT AND JOB BURN-OUT
9. FUNDAMENTALS OF ORGANISZATION PLANNING, DESIGN AND DEVELOPMENT
10. ROLE OF LEADERSHIP IN MANAGEMENT EXCELLENCE

# Table of Contents

6.4 Resources Allocation
6.5 Structuring For Strategy Implementation
6.6 Planning System For Strategy Implementation
6.7 Policies, Plans And Administration
6.8 Plans And Policies
6.9 Integrating Plans And Policies
6.10 Role Of Leadership In Strategy Implementation
6.11 Strategy Implementation In International Settings
6.12 Evaluation And Control Process
6.13 Effectiveness Of Control And Evaluation System
6.14 Criteria For Evaluation
6.15 Performance Measurement And Feedback6.16 Tool For Feedback And Evaluation
6.17 Management By Objectives (Mbo)
6.18 Evaluation And Corrective Action
6.19 Successful Management In Today's Electronic Age
6.20 Building A High–Trust Organization
6.21 Conclding Remarks

7.1 Introduction
7.2 Need for Management Paradigm
7.3 Management from Islamic Perspective
7.4 Ideas Regarding Islamic Perspectives To Strategic Management
7.4.1 Management: Islamic Perspectives
7.4.2 Islamic Management Vs Conventional Management
7.4.3 Operations Management From Islamic Perspective

# FOREWORD

The specific purpose of the "In Search of Management series" is to provide comprensive knowledge, skills, and know-how to students perusing their studies, in general and fields of management/ administration and allied subjects in particular. The series in its totality will provide guideline to all managers at all level from foreman to chief executive engaged in all industries, trade and commerce.

This book in No.2 in the series: "In Search of management Excellence". The book consists of 9 chapters. Chapter 1 consists of introduction. Chapter 2 consists of Corporate Strategy Explained and includes: Introduction; and Corporate Strategy. Chapter 3 consists of Business and Functional Strategies Explained and includes: Introduction; Generic Strategy Approach; Research And Development (R & D) Strategy; Human Resources (HR) Strategy; Organization Design Strategy; Functional Strategy; and Recent Strategic Thinking In Organizational Context During Last Two Decades.

Chapter 4 consists of Strategic Management Process and includes: Introduction; Strategic Management Process, which further includes Formulation Phase Of Strategic Management Process, Implementation Phase Of Strategic Management Process, Evaluation Phase Of Strategic Management Process, Modification Phase Of Strategic Management Process; Strategic Management Elements; Analysis And Diagnosis Of Internal Factors: SWOT Analysis; Factors Influencing Formation Of The Corporate Mission And Objectives; Production And Operations Management Factors; Corporate Resources (Including Personnel) Factors; Marketing And Distribution Factors; Research And Development And Engineering Factors; Finance And Accounting Factors; Analysis And Diagnosis Of The General Environment; The General Environmental

Factors; Socio-Economic, Technological And Governmental Factors, which further includes: Socio-Economic Factors, Technological Factors, and Governmental Factors; Analysis And Diagnosis Of The Industry And International Environment, which further includes: The Industry Environment Factors, Factors Associated With Customer Sector, Associated With Supplier Sector, and the International Environment Factors.

Chapter 5 consists of Choice Of Appropriate Strategy and includes: Generic Strategy Alternatives, which further includes: Stability Strategies; Expansion Strategies; Retrenchment Strategies, and Combination Strategies; and Strategy Variations. Chapter 6 consists of Implementation Of Selected Strategy and includes: Structure And Resources; the Factors That Influence Strategy Implementation, which further includes: Strategy Formulation, Executors, Relationships Among Different Departments And Different Strategy Levels, Adequate Communication Channels, Implementation Tactics, Consensus Within And Outside The Organization, Adequate Organisational Structure, Organizational Administrative Control Systems, and Commitment By All Levels Of Management And By Employees; Implementation Process; Resources Allocation; Structuring For Strategy Implementation; Planning System For Strategy Implementation; Policies, Plans And Administration; Plans And Policies; Integrating Plans And Policies; Role Of Leadership In Strategy Implementation; Strategy Implementation In International Settings; Evaluation And Control Process; Effectiveness Of Control And Evaluation System; Criteria For Evaluation; Performance Measurement And Feedback; Tool For Feedback And Evaluation; Management By Objectives (MBO); Evaluation And Corrective Action; Successful Management in Today's

Electronic Age; Building a High–Trust Organization; and Concluding Remarks.

Chapter 7 consists of Strategic Management From Islamic Perspectives and include: Introduction; Need For Management Paradigm; Management From Islamic Perspective; and Ideas Regarding Islamic Perspectives To Strategic Management, which further includes: Management: Islamic Perspectives, Islamic Management Vs. Conventional Management, and Operations Management From Islamic Perspective. Chapter 8 consists of summary and conclusion. Chapter 9 consists of 25 case stuudies on strategic management The book is supported with bibliography.

However, this book is not intended to be the last word. If the reader wishes to gain a further comprehensive knowledge and deep understanding of the subject matters, he or she is directed to consult scholastic work listed under bibliography and the author feels great pleasure in acknowledging his gratitude to all the authors and publishers of this scholastic work which some times consulted and quoted in the text of this book.

The author earnestly hopes that the matters raised in this book will help the general readers and academic students and scholars and other professional in understanding concepts and application of management, management principles and management process. Finally, the readers and the users of this book are cordially invited to point out errors/mistakes and forward their comments/suggestions, which may bring about improvement to the next edition of this publication.

# Role of Strategic Management in Business Organizations

Praised be to God, the Lord of the Worlds!

Dr Wazir Ali Khan
Senior Citizen of Pakistan and the United Kingdon
Advocate of Peace and Social Reforms Activist
Research Scientist, Author and Publisher
Uxbridge (85) UB7 8AB, London, United Kingdom
Email: drwakhan@aol.com
Published Books link:
http://www.amazon.co.uk/s/ref=nb_sb_noss?url=searc
h-alias%3Ddigital-text&field-keywords=Wazir+Khan

# Chapter 1

## INTRODUCTION

In general, planning is an intellectual process (requiring the use of imagination and sound judgement, etc.), which the executive must carry in order to decide in advance: what is to be done; how and where it is to be done; who will do it; and when to evaluate the results. In other words it is the conscious determination of a course of action to achieve the preconceived goals (objectives) established to guide the efforts of an enterprise.

When a comprehensive plan is aimed at helping the organization to achieve its goals, it is known in general term as strategy. In specific term strategy is a set of actions that an organization plans in response to or in anticipation of changes in its external environment, its customers, its competitors etc. with an aim to improve its competitive position in the market

The researchers have found and come to the conclusion that a well conceived strategy includes four basic components, namely: (a) scope; (b) resource deployment; (c) distinctive competence/competitive advantages; (d) and Synergy. The scope specifies the actual (present) and planned interaction between the organization and its environment. Resource deployment is a vital component of strategy, as resources need to be slanted towards successful operations and away from less successful ones. Competitive advantages resulting from the scope and resource deployment need to be capitalized and this aspect should adequately be specified.

# Role of Strategic Management in Business Organizations

Synergy is the combined action resulting from decisions about organization's scope, resource deployment and competitive advantages and should be taken into account in the strategy formulation and implementation. Strategy formulation is the set of processes involved in determining the strategies of the organization. It determines what the strategy is. Strategy implementation on the other hand is the methods and procedures by which strategies are executed within operation of the organization. It focuses on how strategy is achieved.

Strategy formulation encompasses the set of processes, involved in determining an organization's strategies. These processes include: determination of strategic goals; analysis of the environment; analysis of the organization; and matching the organization with the environment.

F.J. Aguilar[1] suggests that the first step in formulating strategy is to set strategic goals for the organizations. The goals are the broadest in nature established at the organization level. The goals serve to guide the organization's overall strategic direction. The second step in formulating strategy is to conduct an environmental analysis, which in turn involves studying carefully the task environment to identify opportunities available to the organization and also ascertain major threats. The third step in the formulation of strategy is the organizational analysis. The fourth step in the formulation of strategy is matching organizations and environments, in other words matching the strengths

---

[1] Fernando J. Aguilar, author of many books: Editorial Board Member of *Computer Science and Engineering*, Assistant Professor, Universidad de Almería, Spain

and weaknesses of the organization with the corresponding opportunities and threats of the environment.

After strategy is formulated and appropriate planning level is chose then the next step is to implement the strategy which involves understanding the place of planning within the organization, action planning, contingency planning and finally finding a suitable link between strategy and structure of the organization.

Based on strategic planning, the management process of decision making and actions, which determine whether an enterprise excels, survives or dies, is termed as strategic management. In other words strategic management is a stream of decisions and actions, which leads to the development of an effective strategy (or strategies) in helping to achieve corporate objectives. The way in which management (as strategists) determines objectives and makes strategic decisions is termed as the strategic management process.

In this term of reference, strategic decisions are means to achieve ends. These encompass the business definition, products (or service) and markets to be served, functions to be performed, and principal policies needed for the organization or strategic business unit) to execute these decisions. In the text to follow we will describe the role of strategic management in the effective performance of organization.

# Chapter 2

## CORPORATE STRATEGY EXPLAINED

### 2.1    INTRODUCTION

There are many approaches to Corporate Strategy, but the most dominant one is the Business Portfolio Matrix approach to strategy. This approach has its origin at General Electric, but was later developed by the Boston Consulting Group into a complete framework. This approach consists of three phases, namely: (a) identification of strategic business units (SBU), (b) classification of these units into a matrix, and (c) selection of alternative strategies for dealing these units.

Other approaches include intuitive model developed by Steven C. Wheelwright[2]. This approach suggests that managers may determine the paths the organization should follow by developing an intuitive consensus, based on past experience, values, and organization standards and norms. (Hewlett Packard uses this approach.) In planning Corporate Strategy some suggested steps are shown in    Fig. 2.1.

### 2.2    CORPORATE STRATEGY

In a simplest term Corporate Strategy can be defined: "The overall scope and direction of a corporation and the way in which its various business operations work together to achieve particular goals",

---

[2] Steve Wheelwright is the Edsel Bryant Ford Professor of Business Administration, Emeritus at Harvard Business School.

where 'scope' is: the sum of all individual jobs comprising a contract, employment, program, or project; 'corporation' is a business entity formed by filing of Articles of Incorporation and meeting certain legal requirements; 'business operations' are activities involved in the day to day functions of the business conducted for the purpose of generating profits; 'achieve' means (a) to successfully complete tasks, goals or projects - this is often used to describe the act of striving to accomplish something, and (b) reaching for a higher or more coveted status than where initially started, e.g. a director of a company may try to achieve the CEO position; and 'goals' mean an observable and measurable end result having one or more objectives to be achieved within a more or less fixed timeframe.

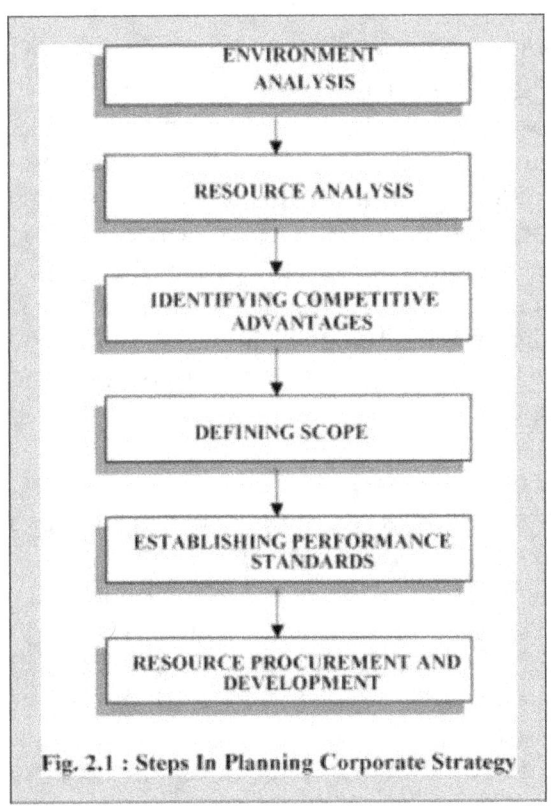

Fig. 2.1 : Steps In Planning Corporate Strategy

# Role of Strategic Management in Business Organizations

According to the classic definition, corporate strategy consists of the actions a company takes to gain competitive advantage. Executives invest enormous energy in product designs and long-range strategic plans, though many of these initiatives become obsolete as markets and competitors adapt, social norms and regulations evolve, and technologies advance. But nevertheless most corporate leaders overlook a golden opportunity to create a durable competitive advantage and generate high returns for less money and with less risk thereby making organizational design the heart of strategy. It's high time for executives to recognize the strategic need to develop organizational capabilities that help companies thrive in all the conditions of od the emerging market.

Modern corporations are massive, complex, dynamic ecosystems and in many of them, organizational inertia is considerable and also organizational design work is hard and time consuming. Therefore, any meaningful change usually involves difficult personality issues and corporate politics, whih inhibit tackling internal organizational issues to boost the performance of companies. It is a common practice that many CEOs typically opt for the ad hoc structural change, the big acquisition, or a focus on where and how to compete instead focusing on organizational design.

The environmental analysis involves the study of the existing products, new products and major threats to the organizations by a close examination of competitors' activities. This analysis also includes monitoring corporate plans, changes in customers' taste, socio-economic changes and analysis of products life cycles in relation to the supply, demand and price characteristics of these products. It should also address finding new opportunities for existing products, finding ways to serve the existing customers with new products or services; and future threats to profitability.

Resource analysis for planning corporate strategy demands an orderly analysis of corporate plans, products, markets, processes, personnel and technology. It involves identifying management competence, strengths in position, technical capabilities, financial status, physical facilities, etc. and also matching present resources against future opportunities. Since the present resources must need to be utilized for a meaningful competitive advantage, resource analysis should adequately address this aspect. Competitive advantages may include: personnel competence, low profit margins (low cost), technological superiority, strong marketing position, strong supply positions, sound financial capabilities, other physical advantages, etc.

Other important concept for planning corporate strategy is the nature of company's overall scope. Clear-cut definition of which product, which customers, and which channel of distribution need to be emphasized to guide and control resource allocation and also to guide corporate management to plan the operation in confidence. To achieve commitment, the goals must be visible and progress measurable. For planning corporate strategy, the performance standards need to be established in the light of company's desired rate of growth, market potential and capacity to survive.

Finally resources procurement and development is an important requisite of planning corporate strategy. It is important in any organization to procure enough trained and qualified personnel to match up the company's growth and steer the strategic direction of the organization. The organization must be conscious of factors such as: the degree of managerial ability, marketing share of the qualified personnel, and competency & growth of the technical and management personnel. It must be understood that unless the organization's corporate resources are procured and deployed in a manner consistent with the competitive advantage, scope of organization, and planning standards, the corporate planning will carry no meaning. Furthermore, the key personnel are needed to carry out strategic program and to optimize the strategic variable such as: pursuing the market segments, offering quality product and services, utilizing the available channel of distribution, following the pricing policy, following financial (investment + expenditure) policy, etc.

The above mentioned concepts of corporate strategy are not sufficient to cope with the needs of the highly changed and developing industrial world and research at the corporate strategic level is continuing to discover new concepts and theories in this regard.

# Chapter 3

## BUSINESS AND FUNCTIONAL STRATEGIES EXPLAINED

## 3.1   INTRODUCTION

Extensive research has been carried out at developing suitable approaches to business level strategy. Two approaches namely 'adaptation model' and 'generic strategies' have been widely used in the industrial world.

Miles and Snow developed the adaptation model approach to business strategy[3]. They identified three basic problems of management, namely: entrepreneurial problem, the engineering problem, and the administrative problem, which need to be addressed simultaneously to match the business goals with opportunities and threats of the environment. In other words, the adaptation model suggests that whilst managing interdependencies, an effective alignment with the organization's environment must also be maintained.

The entrepreneurial problem encounters in defining the organization mission (adding or modifying the existing mix of goals/services/markets/segments for existing business or projections of these for new business). The engineering problem encounters in establishing a system for production, control and distribution of the goods and services identified whilst

---

[3] In their 1978 book *Organization StrategY, Structure, and Process,* Raymond E. Miles and Charles C. Snow argued that different company strategies arise from the way companies decide to address three fundamental problems: entrepreneurial, engineering (or operational), and administrative problems.

solving entrepreneurial problem. The administrative problem encounters whilst developing an appropriate organizational design to achieve the solutions to the entrepreneurial and engineering problems.

For example decisions about decentralization and spans of control are related to administrative problem.

Different organizations approach these problems in different way. However, Miles and Snow[4] have identified four basic approaches, namely defenders organizations, prospectors organizations, analyzer organization and reactors organizations.

Defenders overriding concern is stability of management. Such organizations solve their entrepreneurial problem by keeping a low profile in the market and generally ignoring trends and developments outside their chosen areas; but may employ competitive pricing or high quality standards to protect their positions in the market. These organizations solve their engineering problem by concentrating on efficient production and distribution methods/techniques, but less regard for long-range effectiveness. They solve their administrative problem by maintaining a rigid/bureaucratic form of organization for control and efficiency. The Example of such organizations is publishers, government departments, hospitals, etc.

Prospectors are exactly the opposite of defenders. They are innovators who create and maintain a dynamic environment for themselves in discovering and

---

[4] Miles, Raymond E., and Charles C. Snow. *Organizational Strategy, Structure, and Process.* New York: McGraw-Hill, 1978.

exploiting the new products and markets. They solve their entrepreneurial problem by locating opportunities and then systematically developing these. Prospective organizations solve their engineering problem by finding the ways to avoid a long-term commitment to any single type of technology, and to use several technologies with relatively little routine thus allowing them to shift from product to new product or market to new market without scrapping existing plant and machinery. They solve their administrative problem by finding the way to facilitate rather than to control operation within the organization. The example of such organization is electronic industries.

The analyzers are mid-range organizations in term of their adjustment strategy. They attempt to integrate the strategies of both defenders and prospectors under one organization. They solve their entrepreneurial problem by identifying and taking advantage of new products and markets whilst maintaining full concentration on traditional products and markets. They solve their engineering problem by achieving a balance between the conflicting demands for stability and flexibility in the technology front.

They solve their administrative problem by assigning one group for maintaining the traditional products and markets whilst other in exploring and developing new products and markets. (The example of such organization is cosmetic industries). The adaptation model has much inherent merit. It helps organizations to have better understanding of their respective strategic positions relative to those of other organizations and at the same time it focuses attention on some of the most fundamental problems of management facing today in rather rapidly changing industrial environment.

## 3.2   GENERIC STRATEGY APPROACH

Michael Porter[5] has developed an approach to business strategy known as generic strategy approach. This viewpoint holds that business can adopt three generic strategies, namely: differentiation, overall cost leadership, and focus.   The differentiation strategy focuses on development of an image of product or service, which the customers perceive it as being different than others in the market.   The product or service may have special attributes e.g., quality, design, after sale service, etc., which could be readily differentiated in terms of those attributes.

By using this strategy the organization can charge higher prices and consequently make more profits by offering a unique product.   Overall cost leadership strategy guides the organizations in attempting to maximize sales by charging lower unit price as a result of minimizing cost.   The third generic strategy (focus) suggests successfully focusing products or services on specific segments of the total market with less emphasis on keeping lower prices.

## 3.3   RESEARCH AND DEVELOPMENT (R & D) STRATEGY

Most people perceive of R & D, as it is the part of the company that is responsible for inventing new products, but nevertheless this is equally important even for further developing existing products because consumer preferences constantly change.

---

[5] Porter, M. E.: Competitive Strategy (New York: Free Press, 1985).

Accordingly, the chief job of product research and development is to come up with goods and services that meet the changing needs of the consumers of tomorrow,

## 3.4 HUMAN RESOURCES (HR) STRATEGY

HR Stategy is considered in simple terms 'Staffing' as it is putting a policy in place for the the areas, such as: (a) recruitement - how do you recruite the best employees; (b) retain - how to keep the best employees; (c) termination - how to terminate poor employees; and (d) how do we learn from' good employees leaving. In this context, recruitement activities include: how do we perform interviews - (standardized/subjective); where do we post - (Ask current employees, job boards, headhunter,etc) ; what criteria do we establish - (random drug screens, personality tests, etc.)

HR Strategy is aligning the goals of HR to the goals or strategy of an organisation whereas recruitment, retention and termination are a small part of it. In developing a HR strategy two critical questions must be addressed.: (a) what kinds of people do you need to manage and run a business to meet ones strategic business objectives; and (b) what people programs and initiatives must be designed and implemented to attract, develop and retain staff to compete effectively? In order to answer these questions four key dimensions of an organization must be addressed: (i) organization culture ( encompassing: the beliefs, values, norms and management style of the organization); (ii) organization (encompassing the structure, job roles and reporting lines of the organization); (iii) people in the organization (encompassing: the skill levels, staff potential and management capability); and (iv) human resources systems (encompassing: the people focused mechanisms which deliver the strategy - employee selection, communications, training, rewards, career development, etc.

## 3.5   ORGANIZATION DESIGN STRATEGY

The dynamics of the environment and the readiness of organizations to understand and adapt to the demands of the market, make a difference between success and failure. In organizational term, since strategy is an action plan for developing core competences to reach long-term goals and gain a competitive advantage, when core competences stem from specialized resources possessed by functional personnel, organizational resources, and coordination abilities; therefore strategies that create value and achieve competitive advantage are formulated at four levels, namely: (a) functional level; (b) business level; (c) corporate level; and (d) global level.

Achieving a competitive advantage at the functional level means gaining a low-cost or adifferentiation advantage, thereby interorganizational strategies, such as long-term contracts, develop functional resources and coordination abilities, which strengthen core competences; whilst contingency theory examines differences in structural design among the R&D, manufacturing, and sales functions, while culture affects functional-level strategy. Business-level strategy combines functional level core competences to protect the organizational domain, e.g. two business-level strategies are differentiation and low cost. In this context there are four strategies that enlarge the organizational domain, namely: (a) market penetration; (b) product development; (c) market development; and (d) diversification. Organizational structure and culture, however, must match business-level strategy.

Other organizational structures include: product; market; geographic; product team; and matrix. A low-cost organization, however, needs cultural values of economy, whereas a differentiator needs values of innovation and quality. Traditional organizations that are unable to understand and manage change, have higher difficulty to find their path to success (Drazin & Howard, 1984)[6].

## 3.6  FUCTIONAL STRATEGY

This strategy primarily determines how activities in each of the organizational functional areas will support the business strategy by specifying activities within respective functional area within an organization, such as marketing, finance, legal, etc. This level of strategy, by and large, derives the operational goals and plans that are the means for achieving tactical goals in the hierarchy of goals of the organization's planning process. Such a strategy is typically developed by middle management that heads up the respective functional area, and it often tends to focus on short term basis i.e. up to one year or so.

## 3.7  RECENT STRATEGIC THINKING IN ORGANIZATIONAL CONTEXT DURING LAST TWO DECADES

**1992 :** The CEO as organization designer, 'in an interview with Prof. Jay W. Forrester' conclded that: " in a complex world, to "design" means to rethink the logic of cause and effect."

**1993:** In February, on the question on 'think local, organize … question, new evidence suggested that the most popular routes to global success are not

---

[6] Drazin, R, Howard, P. 1984. Strategy Implementation: A Technique for Organizational Design. *Columbia Journal of World Business* 19, 40–46

always reliable, whilst in August on 'balancing corporate power' a new federalist paper (winner of the McKinsey Award for the best article) published in the Harvard Business Review in 1992 provided answer to - how complex modern organizations can achieve unity without uniformity.

**1994:** In May on Fallacies in organizing for performance, a brief introduction to the most common assumptions that lead astray efforts to boost performance was provided.

**1996:** In February on the question: what is wrong with the consumer goods organization, a new category-based structure was born, whist in August two companies (Ford and Kraft) got it right 'flatness forays' on reorganizing around processes and finding the answetr to the question: how much functional structure should be left in place?

**1998:** In February on ' the new economics of organization' in their purest forms, the coordination of markets motivate and hierarchies, the technique to combine the best of both were achieved, thereby accepting the two challenges for the corporations of the future: entrepreneurialism and knowledge.

**1999:** In Noevember, through the dialog: 'can a company ever be too big', conflictiong views emerged as some people believed that "it is different this time." Others did'nt.

**2001:** In February on 'beyond the business unit', it was recognized that corporate organization's future lied in the ability to work across business units and concluded that opportunity-based organizational design may help to achieve success. In May on 'organization growth', as drivers of corporate success, organizational design and the quality of leadership shared pride of place with strategy, wholst 'the innovative organization'the trick was found to balance partitioning and integration in answer to the question: how new companies can grow quickly without sacrificing performance discipline. In August, on 'beyond the unbundled corporation'it was realized that a new business model may forever change the way companies compete; whilst on 'making solution the answer', many companies hard-pressed to maintain their margins through products alone are turning to 'solutions.' But to succeed, they must not only embrace competitors but also often turn away existing customers; and on managing the knowledge manager', it was discovered than before developing and executing agenda, it is imperative to agree on what you want to achieve. In the same month on 'the future of the network company', it was found that even during the slowdown, networked companies outperforming conventional ones with prospectus to go on doing so.

**2002:** In June, on 'Just-in-time strategy for a turbulent world', uncertainty and rising levels of risk made it impossible for companies to determine the future and found out that a portfolio-of-initiatives approach to strategy can help ensure that companies take full advantage of their best opportunities without taking unnecessary risks. In December 2002 on ' who is accouuntavle for IT, it was found that who were business leaders.

**2003:** In June, on ' knowledge management comes to philanthropy', ir was found that Foundations were endowed with intellectual as well as financial capital, thereby then was the time to use it. On 'organization helping people pull together', it was fond that even in the largest and best-managed companies, hundreds of organizational muddles took place every day, who throughout the economy, added up to a staggering waste of national resources.

On, 'organizational lessons for nonprofits', America learned the importance of building organizational capacity the hard way. On, 'the value in organization',it was established that CEOs must be more architect than general and took the tasks to design working environments where thousands of people know what to do, cooperate to get it done, and experience it as personally fulfilling. On, 'when reorganization works, it was realized that even a corporate revamping inspired by state-of-the-art design principles won't succeed if not driven by a powerful, well-timed business idea adapted to social realities.

In August on 'managing for improved corporate performance', generating great performance required a more dynamic approach to building and adapting a company's capabilities than merely squeezing its operations. On. 'what CEOs really think about IT',it was found that executives in France were taking a more proactive approach to ensure their IT investments bear fruit.

**2004:** in March on 'when efficient capital and operations go hand in hand', Olli-Pekka Kallasvuo, Nokia's head of mobile phones and a former CFO, discussed strategic organization, performance measurement, and the value of financial transparency. In July on, 'next-generations CIOs', to ensure that IT investments have the greatest impact, CIOs must involve business-unit leaders and concentrate on the big picture.

In August on 'making a market in knowledge', it was determined that for companies and their employees alike, knowledge is power—and profit; whilst on' 'on organizing Customer Relationship Management (CRM)',it was determined that companies should treat a CRM solution as a product or service and its users as internal customers, by making it valuable, pricing appropriately, advertising, and providing after-sales support.In Novemeber on, 'organizing for effectiveness in public sector', it was found that traditional public-sector organizations can be redesigned to perform more successfully—even when market forces are lacking.

**2005:** In February on 'leadership as the starting point of strategy', it was found that even the best strategy can fail if a corporation doesn't have a cadre of leaders with the right capabilities at the right levels of the organization. In April on 'how to escape the short-term trap',it was determined that markets may expect solid performance over the short term, but they also value sustained performance over the long term, therby companies managing both time frames. In May on. 'global champions from emerging markets, it was found that developing economies had become an invaluable springboard for companies looking to compete successfully in foreign market. In July on, 'it was found that according to the McKinsey Global Survey of Business Executives, confidence was down, whilst distractions were up. In August on. 'building the healthy corporation',it was found that it wass difficult—but vital—for managers to strike a balance between the short and long terms strategies. In the same month on 'getting bigger' it was found that the world's largest companies were more successful than ever, but scale bringing its own challenges.

In the same month on, 'the 21$^{st}$-century organizatios', it was found that big corporations must make sweeping organizational changes to get the best from their professionals. In the same month on, 'what its leaders do' it was found that companies that relied on IT governance systems alone will come up short. In November on,'improving productivity', it wad found that economic activity in developed economies was again undergwent a broad and deep shift; whilst on, 'strategy in an era of global giants', it was found that the world's biggest companies were learning to manage complexity; and on, 'the next revolution in interaction', it was found that successful efforts to exploit the growing importance of complex interactions could well generate durable competitive advantages.

**2006:** In Januuary on, 'ten trends to watch', it was found that macroeconomic factors, environmental and social issues, and business and industry developments will all profoundly shape the corporate landscape in the coming years. In February on, 'distortions and deceptions in strategic decisions', it was found that companies were vulnerable to misconceptions, biases, and plain old lies, but not hopelessly vulnerable; and on, 'the 'moment of truth' in customer service', it was found that focus on the interactions that are important to customers—and on the way frontline employees handled those interactions and executives should recognize and compensate for cognitive biases and agency problem; and on, 'the right service strategies for product companies', it was found that as products evolved into commodities, services became more important, but however, companies that play this new game must understand its rules; whist on, it was found that 'when organization isn't enough restructuring doesn't always lead to improved performance.

In April on 'an executive take on the top budiness trendsL a McKinsey Global Survet', it was found that executives reported an accelerating pace of change in an increasingly competitive business environment, driven by knowledge and information trends and the forces of globalization. In May on, 'competitive advantage from better interaction', it was found that tacit interactions are becoming central to economic activity, thereby making those who undertake them more effective isn't like tweaking a production line; whilst on. 'making a market in talent', it was found that a $21^{st}$-century company should put as much effort into developing its talented employees as it puts into recruiting them; and on, 'the adaptable corporation', it was found that to survive, organizations must execute in the present and adapt to the future and it was also found that only few of organizations manage to do both well.

In July on, 'building a nimble organization: a McKinsey Global Survey', it was found that executives saw an urgent need to increase the agility and speed of their organization and were trying in various ways to do so. In Agust on managing your organizations by the evidence', it was found that an organization was much more likely to improve its current performance and underlying health by using a combination of complementary practices rather than any one of them alone, according to new McKinsey research.

In August, 'on mapping the value of employee collaboration', as collaboration within and among organizations became increasingly important, and recommended that companies must improve their management of the networks where it typically occurs. In September on improving strategic planning: a McKinsey Survey', it was found that executives pointed out that their companies could be a lot more effective at developing a strategy and implementing strategic plans, whilst suggesting some areas for improvement. In November on, 'managing for growth: an interview with former Emerson CEO Chuck Knight', it was determined that the company's CEO from 1973 to 2000 explained how it transformed itself from a local manufacturer of simple components into a global technology giant.

**2007:** In January on what public companies can learn from private equity', it was found that Public companies will need to raise their governance game if they are to compete with private firms. In April on, ' acting on global trends: A McKinsey Global Survey', it was found that executives saw opportunities as well as risks in the global business landscape, yet many were not addressing them; whilst on, 'the role of networks in organizational change', it was found that companies shouldn't focus so much on formal structures while ignoring the informal ones.

In May on, 'anatomy of a healthy corporation', it was found necessary to know the answer to the question: how can business leaders embed "healthy" thinking in the organization? Also on, 'better strategy through organizational design', it was found that redesigning an organization to take advantage of today's sources of wealth creation wasn't easy, but there can be no better use of a CEO's time; whilst on, 'building the civilized workplace', it was found that nasty people did not just make others feel miserable but also they created economic problems for their companies; and on, 'cracking the complexity code', it was found that there were two types of complexity and to manage them to creat value, understanding where to intervene is the key; whilst on, 'managing in a complex world', it was found that creating value from the challenges complexity presents was a major challenge confronting today's companies.

In July on, 'better strategy for business uuunit: a McKinsey Survey', it was found that executives were most positive about the outcomes of strategy formulation for their companies' business units when they work at companies that use a collaborative approach, and while they say following best practices yields better results, they use those practices less often than they think they should. In August on, 'connecting employees to create value in investment banks' it was found that leaders used to have few options for changing their companies, except focusing on financial performance and walking the halls, which was no longer true; whilst on, 'the link between profit and organizational performance', McKinsey research indicated that organizational and financial performance were strongly mutually related.

In September on spurring value creation in IT services: an interviewing with the chairman of Indea's Satyan Computers', the founder and chairman of Satyam detailed the philosophy that has underpinned the company's rapid ascent through the ranks of the world's top IT services providers. In November on, ' harnessing the power of informal employee networks', it was found that  formalizing a company's ad hoc peer groups can spur collaboration and unlock value; whilst on, 'innovative management: A conversation with Gary Hamel and Lowell Bryan', it was determined that forward-looking executives must respond to the growing need for a new managerial model.

**2008:** In January on 'Peter L. Bernstein on risk, the celebrated author of 'Against the Gods': The Remarkable Story of Risk explored the history of risk and how it worked in real-world markets and in our lives. In April on, the promise of prediction markets: a roundtable discussion it was found that although they drew together widely dispersed information, prediction markets faced organizational and legal challenges. In

## Role of Strategic Management in Business Organizations

May on what are the design flaws in your organization', Gary Hamel and the Management Lab explored improving performance by rethinking organizational structure; whilst on, 'in an interview with Daniel Kahneman on behaviour economics, the Nobel Laureate said that organizations should think of decisions like any other product, and apply quality controls.

In July on, 'managing capital projects: lesions from Asia', it was found that some Asian companies were better at executing capital projects than were rivals elsewhere. What lessons can others learn from them? Al on. 'from internal service provider to strategic partner; an interview with the head of Global Business services at P&G, it was found that Filippo Passerini wass bringing the back office into the boardroom. In September on, 'a bsiness case for women', it was found that the gender gap was not just an image problem: research suggested that it can have real implications for company performance.

Some companies had taken effective steps to achieve greater parity. In December on, 'a fresh look at strategy under uncertainty: an interview', it was determined that although even the highest levels of uncertainty did not prevent businesses from analyzing predicaments rationally, said author Hugh Courtney, "the financial crisis has shown us the limits of our tools—and minds"; whilst on ' leading through uncertainity', it was found that the range of possible futures confronting business was great. Companies that nurtured flexibility, awareness, and resiliency are more likely to survive the crisis, and even to prosper; and on, 'manging regulation in a new era', it was found that as concern over global problems mounte, executives and regulators had everything to gain from building relationships based on trust, and developing solutions that benefit a wide range of stakeholders.

**2009:** In Febrary on, 'the crises: mobilizing board for change', it was founs that to meet the challenges of the economic crisis, corporate boards must change the way they work; whilst on, 'when clinician lead', it was found that health care systems that were serious about transforming themselves must harness the energies of their clinicians as organizational leaders. In May on, 'improving performance at state-owned enterprises', it was found that public-sector companies can match the performance of their private-sector counterparts and even become world-class players. In August on 'unlocking the potential of fronline managers', it was found that instead of administrative work and meetings, frontline managers should focus on coaching their employees and on constantly improving quality.

In December on, 'competing through organizational agility', three distinct types of agility—strategic, portfolio, and operational—help companies compete, with each of them having its own sources and dangers; whilst on, ' dynamic managementLbetter decisions in uncertain time', it was found that companies can't predict the future, but they can build organizations that will survive and flourish under just about any possible future.

**2010:** In January on, 'the five attributes of enduring family businesses', it was found that the keys to long-term success were professional management and keeping the family committed to and capable of carrying on as the owner. In February on, ' how companies manage the front line today: McKinsey Survey resuults', it was found that most companies did not offer sufficient training for frontline managers or structure their roles to create the most value.

## Role of Strategic Management in Business Organizations

Aggravating the problem, senior leaders were often unaware of the issues that hinder frontline performance. Companies with effective frontline managers took a different approach.

In March on, 'building organizational capabilities: McKinsey Global Survey reslts' it was found that building organizational capabilities, such as leadership development or lean operations, is a top priority for most companies, but many of them have not yet figured out how to do so effectively. The odds improved at companies where senior leaders were more involved. In April on, a new world for brand managers', it was found that CPG companies had created fragmented, overlapping structures that prevented brand and category managers—and the companies themselves— from achieving their full potential. In May on, 'putting organizational complexity in its place', it was found that not all complexity is bad for business—but executives did not always know what kind their company has. They should understand what creates complexity for most employees, remove what doesn't add value, and channel the rest to employees who can handle it effectively.

In September on, 'boosting the productivity of knowledge workers' it was found that the key is identifying and addressing the barriers workers face in their daily interactions; whilst on, 'creating value in the age of distributed capitalism', it was found that as mass consumption gave way to the wants of individuals, a historic transition in capitalism wass unfolding; and on, thing beyondthe pblic company', it was found that mutualization and partnerships were once common ownership structures in finding the answer to the question: could they once again limit financial risks effectively?

In November on, 'beyond paid media: marketing new vocabulary', it was found that changes to the way consumers perceive and absorb marketing messages will force marketers to change not only their thinking but also the way they allocate spending and organize operations; whilst on, dispatches from the front lines of management innovation', it was found that in meeting the M-Prize winners—three case studies in management innovation honored by Gary Hamel's Management Innovation exchange; and on, 'Mckinsey conversations with global leaders: Jim Owen of Catterpillat', it was found that Caterpillar's former chairman and CEO reflected on an unconventional career path, organizational change, and how and where to stay competitive over the long term. In December on, 'the rise of the networked enterprise: McKinsey's new survey research found that companies using the Web intensively gained greater market share and higher margins.

**2011:** In January on, 'the question: is your top team undermining your supply chain', it was found that building bridges between senior managers is a critical step in constructing tomorrow's global supply chain. In February on, 'rethinking knowledge work: a strategic approach' it was found that knowledge workers information needs varied, thereby implying that the key to better productivity is applying technology more precisely. In March on, 'question for your HR chief: are we using our people data to create value', it was found that by analyzing the links between people practices and productivity, some companies were improving their bottom line; whilst on, 'seven steps to better brainstorming' it was found that most attempts at brainstorming were doomed, thereby to generate better ideas—and boost the odds that organization will act on them—started by asking better questions.

## Role of Strategic Management in Business Organizations

In Apri on, 'sparking creativity in teams: an executive's guide', it was found that senior managers can apply practical insights from neuroscience to make themselves—and their teams—more creative. In May on, 'Eric Schmidt on business culture, technology, and social issue', it was found that Google's executive chairman shares his strategies on hiring, running meetings, designing "mobile first" business models, and addressing joblessness and education reform; and on preparing your organization for growth', it was found that companies that addressed their organizational weaknesses as they implemented growth strategies gave themselves an advantage.

In June on, 'organizational heath:the ultimate competitive advantage', it was found that to sustain high performance, organizations must build the capacity to learn and keep changing over time; whilst on, 'the perils of bad strategy', it was found that bad strategy abounds, UCLA management professor Richard Rumelt pointed out  that senior executives who can spot it stand a much better chance of creating good strategies; whilst on, ' to the question: to centralize or not to centralize', it was found that it's  a hard call made harder by power struggles, thereby CEOs can force a more thoughtful debate by asking three critical questions. In July on, 'understanding your globalization penalty`, it was found that strong multinationals seemed less healthy than successful companies that stuck closer to home.

In September on, 'changing companies' minds about women', it was found that leaders who were serious about getting more women into senior management needed a hard-edged approach to overcome the invisible barriers holding them back; whilst on, 'social technologies on the frontline: the management 2.0 M-Prize winners, it was found that executives who won a contest McKinsey cosponsored with Gary Hamel's Management Innovation eXchange (MIX) and the Harvard Business Review highlighted myriad ways Web 2.0 was improving communication among employees at all levels.

**2012:** In January on, 'how leaders kill meaning at work', it was found that senior executives routinely undermined creativity, productivity, and commitment by damaging the inner work lives of their employees in four avoidable ways. In March on, 'how multinational can winn in India', it was found that companies should avoid simply imposing global business models and practices on the local market; whilst on, 'listening to employees: the 'Beyond Bureaucracy' M-Prize winners', it was found that seven winning entries in a contest McKinsey cosponsored with Gary Hamel's Management Innovation eXchange (MIX) and Harvard Business Review revealed executive thinking on the importance of engaging employees in an open and realistic way; and on, 'the power of an independent corporate center', it was found that to develop a winning corporate strategy, you may need more muscle in your headquarters.

In May on, the social side of strategy', it was found that crowdsourcing your strategy may sound crazy, but a few pioneering companies were starting to do just that, boosting organizational alignment in the process. In June on, leading in the 21$^{st}$ century', it was found that six global leaders confronted the personal and professional challenges of a new era of uncertainty; whilst on managing at global scale: McKinsey Global Survey results', it was found that executives at global companies were satisfied with their organizations' overall capabilities while seeing room to improve in innovation and motivation, tereby concluding that better leaders are the key.

# Role of Strategic Management in Business Organizations

Also in June on, 'organizing for an emerging world', it was found that the structures, processes, and communications approaches of many far-flung businesses had been stretched to the breaking point in the wake of some ideas for relieving the strains; whilst on, 'the global company's challenge', it was found that 1992 as the economic spotlight shifted to developing markets, global companies needed new ways to manage their strategies, people, costs, and risks.

In September on, 'encouraging your people to take the long view', it was found that employees and managers should be measured as much on their contribution to an organization's long-term health as to its performance. In Novemeber on, 'the evolution of work: one company's story' it has been found that Symantec's chief human-resources officer, Rebecca Ranninger, describes the security software company's transition to a virtual workplace while reflecting on the promise—and perils—of new ways of working.

# Chapter 4

## STRATEGIC MANAGEMENT PROCESS

### 4.1 INTRODUCTION

Strategic management forms the core of any business management. It is the ongoing process of formulating and implementing comprehensive plans and policies (through a process that provides a framework for examining the organizational environment, for developing and implementing strategy, and for responding to organizational changes) that help organizations to fulfil their corporate missions and achieve their strategic goals.

Strategic management requires the strategists to formalise objectives, formally assess where their enterprises' strengths and weakness are, and formally assess events in the environment to identify opportunities and threats. However, ability to formulate plans and policies (which are needed to implement the grand strategy) will be a good indication of practical implications to make the strategy to work. Researchers have suggested that the success of an enterprise's strategy is dependent on proper implementation and balancing of resources, and integrated plans and policies.

### 4.2 STRATEGIC MANAGEMENT PROCESS

The strategic management process in an organization (i.e. a strategic business unit) is shown in Fig.2.2. The process follows four distinct phases as follows, namely: (a) formulation; (b) implementation; (c) evaluation; and (d) modification.

### 4.2.3 Formulation Phase of Strategic Management Process

Strategic management process begins with the formulation phase, where the firm's management develops an overall strategy for achieving the firm's overall objectives, where objectives may include, for example, increasing market share or reducing costs. It is responsibility of the top management to develop the enterprize's overall strategy, but the top management may, however, seek the input of line managers and front-line workers as they develop their strategy.

### 4.2.2 Implementation Phase of Strategic Management Process

The management then, with a clear strategy formulated, can go about implementing it. Strategies are, by and large, implemented from the top down through middle management to lower level management. To begin with implementation, the top management, through the middle management will inform line managers about the strategic changes, and line managers, in turn, will pass this information on to their subordinates. Many strategies often fail due to poor implementation, but the top management can avoid this by carefully introducing the new strategy and listening to the employees concern about the changes.

### 4.2.4 Evaluation Phase of Strategic Management Process

Although, when a strategy is implemented, it will hopefully be successful, but nevertheless the managerment cannot assume that every strategy will work, therefore evaluation mechanism must be in place so that the success of the strategy is measured against the datum set my the top management. In other words to measure this success, the strategy must be evaluated against the firm's goals and objectives. In this respect a gap analysis is a very useful, i.e. gap analysis measures the gap that exists between the desired results and a enterprize's actual results.

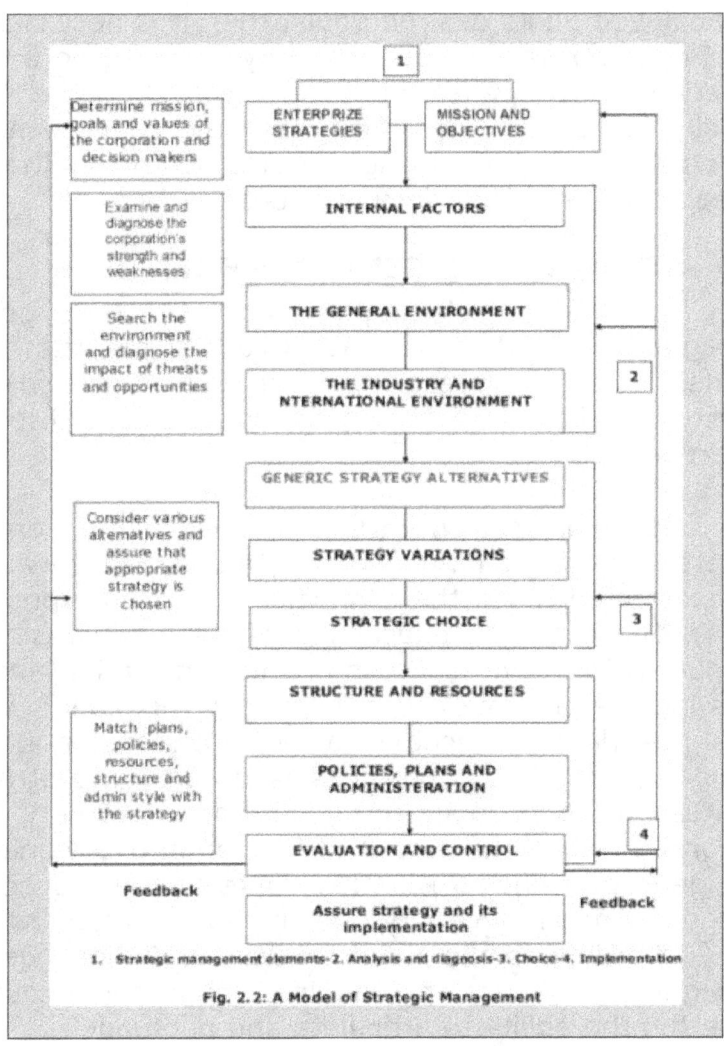

Fig. 2.2: A Model of Strategic Management

## 4.2.5 Modification Phase of Strategic Management Process

Very often carefully formulated strategies meet success on the first attempt, but nevertheless more often than not, there is room for improvement. If the evaluation of the strategy shows that the enterprize has not achieved all its desired goals, then it is necessary to modify the strategy, e.g. if the enyerprize used a cost-leadership strategy to increase sales, but the sales actually decreased, then the firm would need to modify this strategy, perhaps using a premium-pricing strategy instead originally formulated stretegy.

## 4.3 STRAGIC MANAGEMENT ELEMENTS

The key elements include (i) general management, (ii) corporate-level strategists, (iiii) business level strategies, and (iv) mission and objectives. These are shown in Fig. 2.3 and discussed herein below:

**General Management:** The Managers are key players in strategic management process as they are the top exececutives at the pinnacle of the enterprise (or SBUs). These are the executives who are responsible for the survival and the success of the corporation and thir titles include chairman, vice chairman, president, senior vice president, executive vice president and vice president, etc. If the business is divided into strategic business units or operating divisions of a very large corporation, then the person at the top of these units are also general managers in this context. Such a general mangemer needs a variety of skill and has many roles to play. According to the Havard Business School, general management leadership "requires judgement, courage, empathy, the ability to articulate and persuade"

**Corporate-Level Strategists:** The directors of the board and chief executive officers are primarily the players involved in making corporate-level strategy. In family owned business or small enterprise, the entrepreneur is both the general manager and chief strategist. However, the role of chief executive officer (CEO) is crucial to the success of the strategic management, being responsible for defining what business the company is in and matching the best product-market opportunities with optimum use of the company's resources. Therefore, the CEO must conceptualise the strategic direction of the company and take initiative in installing and maintaining the strategic management process.

**Business-Level Strategists:** These fall in four groups, namely: operational managers (SBU managers), corporate planners, consultants and lower-level managers. The operation managers perform roles as business strategists by attempting to get best results in their business segment given their resources and corporate objectives. Corporate planners are assigned with vital functions of providing technical back up and service as executive research and follow-through as an aid in making strategic decisions by the general and corporate management.

Consultant in strategic management also plays a vital role as he is expert in designing a formal strategic management system for an enterprise and he can also help in its implementation. Their role is particularly more useful and cost effective for small and medium size companies who are not having in-house corporate planners in their organizations. Lower-Level Managers, although are not intimately involved with strategic choice, but are important players in providing data or ideas which can affect future choices at higher levels and also implement plans and policies consistent with strategic intent.

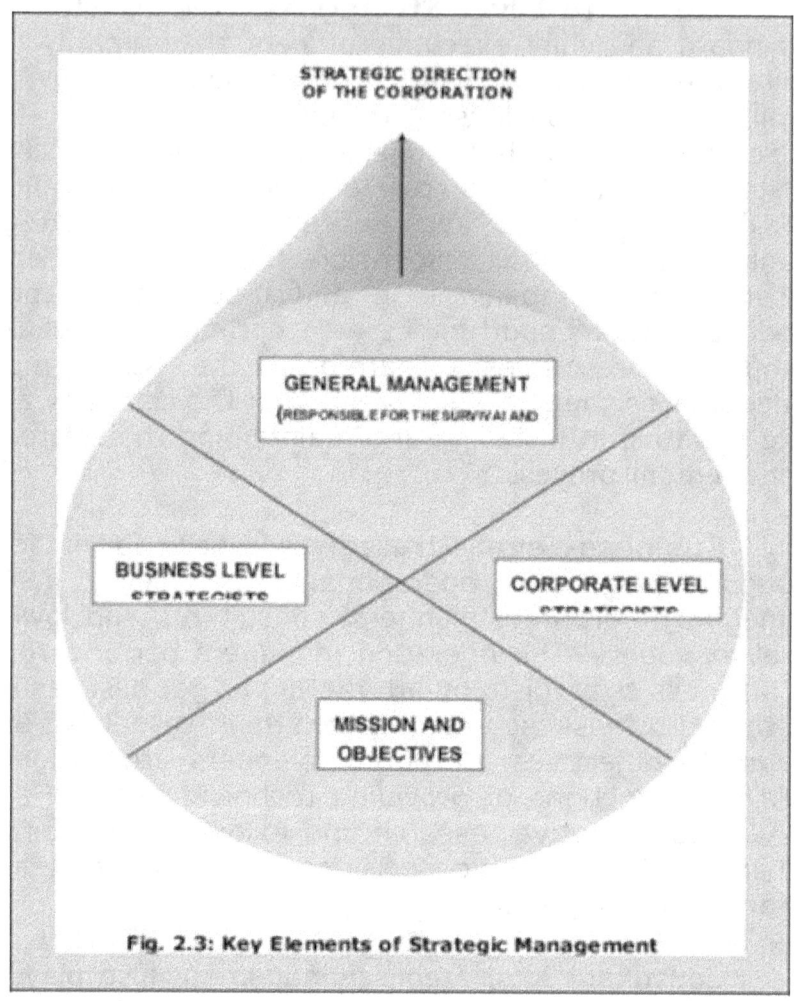

STRATEGIC DIRECTION
OF THE CORPORATION

GENERAL MANAGEMENT
(RESPONSIBLE FOR THE SURVIVAI AND

BUSINESS LEVEL
STRATEGISTS

CORPORATE LEVEL
STRATEGISTS

MISSION AND
OBJECTIVES

Fig. 2.3: Key Elements of Strategic Management

**Mission and Objectives:** Clearly defined mission and objectives are fundamental to the formulation of an organization strategy. It is important to know what business we are in (mission) and why we are in that busies (objectives to be accomplished). Many entrepreneurs across the globe define the basic reason for their being in business in the form of a mission statement and communicating it at all levels of their organizations. The mission must be clearly defined so that it leads to desired action. For example, in 1960 when John F. Kennedy proclaimed his desire to put the man on the moon then the authority who was made responsible for the program (NASA) was charged with the mission 'to begin space exploration and land a man on the moon'. An other example in this context can be cited about General Motors. Immediately after Roger Smith took over as a chairman of General Motors, he distributed "cultural cards" to executives with an instruction to be carried in their pockets to remind them of their new mission. The text of the cards read:

*"The fundamental purpose of General Motors is to provide products and services of such quality that our customers will receive superior value, our employees and business partners will share in our success, and our stockholders will receive a sustained, superior return on their investment"*

However, mission statement is neither a day to day concern of decision making process nor a set of platitudes, but it ought to serve as guidelines for strategic decisions.

Objectives (or goals, as the terms are used synonymously) are the ends which the organization seeks to achieve through its existence and operations. Each business organization would have a variety of different objectives to pursue, some on short run, some on medium range and some on long run basis. For example, many companies may view employees satisfaction and efficiency as short run objectives, profit continuity, good corporate culture and service to society as long run objectives whilst asset control or adaptability as medium-range objectives. It is therefore an important task of strategists to give a time weight to the pursuance of these objectives and establish priorities for each objective at corporate as well as SBU levels. It is important to note that the clearly defined objectives are vital strategic management requisites because of many reasons, such as (a) objectives help to define the organization in its environment, (b) objectives helps in the co-ordination process, (c) objectives provide standards for assessing organizational performance, and (d) objectives are more tangible targets than mission statements.

Because of their inherent importance, mission and objectives ought to be considered at each stage of the strategic management process. To assure success of the strategic management process, it is vital for the corporate strategists to formulate them well and communicate them throughout the enterprise and equally vital for the general management to see that these reflect the values of management and the realities of the prevailing situation of the organization. The formulation of mission and objectives, however, is a complex process because of many factors influencing the formulation process. Four major such factors are shown in Fig. 2.4. Each of these factors represents a set of constraints on the establishment of priorities among future objectives. These factors also play a vital role in strategic choice. In the formulation of mission and objectives apart from these four factors the consideration of gaps analysis between desired and expected goal attainments is also important.

## 4.4 ANALYSIS AND DIAGNOSIS OF INTERNAL FACTORS: SWOT ANALYSIS

Internal analysis is the process by which strategists examine the internal factors such as: production and operations; corporate resources including personnel, marketing and distribution; research and development; engineering; and finance and accounting, etc. to determine where the enterprise has significant strengths and weaknesses. Internal diagnosis is the process by which strategists determine how to exploit the opportunities and meet the threats by using strength to the optimum level and minimising and repairing weakness in order to build sustainable competitive advantages.

It is a fact that every enterprize (as well as each division within an enterprize) has strengths and weaknesses and, therefore it is important for the executives to regularly analyse their weaknesses and be aware of their competitive advantages if they wish to choose one opportunity out of many available at the time which would likely to lead to the greatest success and also to face the environment threats most effectively. Likewise, it is equally important to regularly analyse the environment so that decision can be made about how to use to the optimum or add strengths and minimise weaknesses.

This process is in fact composite and as a whole generally termed as SWOT Analysis. This process involves the management to perform internal analysis and diagnosis to identify the current strengths and weaknesses and also to examine the most probable future strengths and weaknesses. On the basis of these assessments, expectations are developed about goal attainment under given conditions (external and internal), and if gaps are identified between desired and expected objectives, new strengths are developed or weaknesses preventing goal attainment are overcome.

## 4.5 FACTORS INFLUENCING FORMATION OF THE CORPORATE MISSION AND OBJECTIVES

These factors are shown in Fig. 2.4

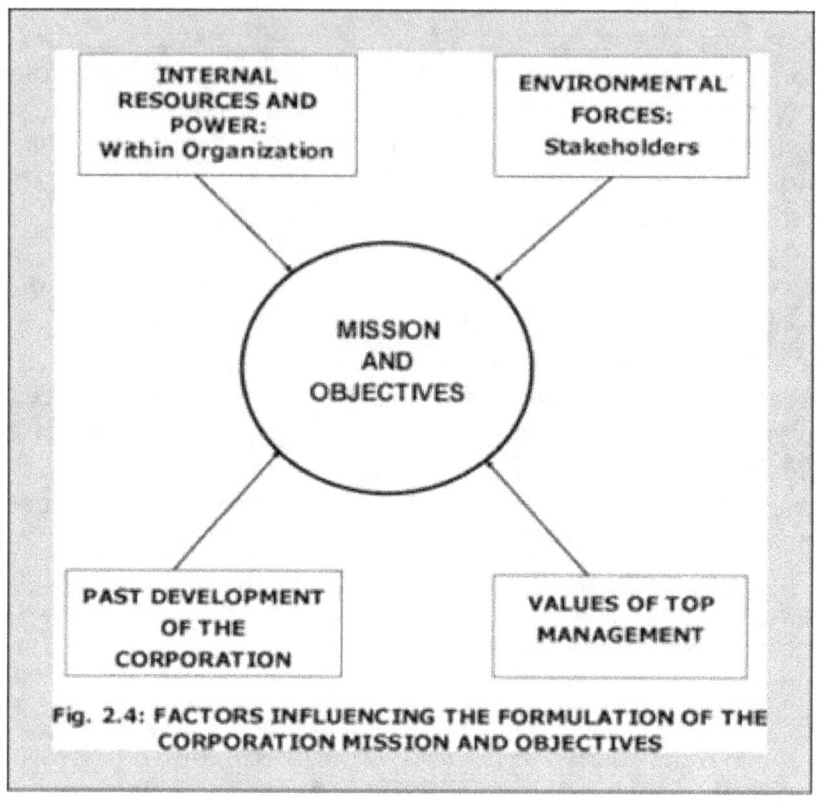

Fig. 2.4: FACTORS INFLUENCING THE FORMULATION OF THE CORPORATION MISSION AND OBJECTIVES

## 4.6  PRODUCTION AND OPERATIONS MANAGEMENT FACTORS

For analysing production and operations the following factors should be considered as a checklist.

➤ Total operations cost as compared to competitors' total costs.
➤ Capacity to meet market demands.
➤ Cost effective and efficient facilities.
➤ Costs of raw materials and subassemblies.
➤ Availability of raw materials and subassemblies.
➤ Cost effective and efficient machinery and equipment.

➢ Effective and efficient inventory control systems.
➢ Cost effective and efficient design of the plant.
➢ Effective planning, scheduling, quality control and procedures.
➢ Cost effective and efficient production methods and controls.
➢ Cost effective and efficient maintenance policies and procedures.
➢ Flexibility in operational activities.
➢ Effective working relations with suppliers.
➢ Effective vertical and horizontal integration.
➢ Strategic location of facilities and offices.
➢ Effective and efficient offices.

Note: By carefully considering the above factors and bringing regular improvements when possible will no doubt give the enterprise a competitive advantage.

## 4.7 CORPORATE RESOURCES (INCLUDING PERSONNEL) FACTORS

This is a very important area, which should be carefully analysed. The following factors should be considered as a checklist.

➢ Corporate prestige and image in the market places.
➢ Effective organization design, structure, climate and culture.
➢ Optimum size in relation to the industry to avoid barrier to entry.
➢ Strategic management system.
➢ Management information and computer systems (potent strategic weapons).
➢ Manuals, operational procedures and work instructions.
➢ Effective corporate-staff systems.
➢ Effective hiring policy and selection of high quality employees.

- ➢ Effective management selection with balanced experience and track record.
- ➢ Cost effective labour as measured by remuneration, turnover and absenteeism.
- ➢ Effective and efficient personnel relations and incentives policies.
- ➢ Effective public relations including relation with trade unions (if applicable).
- ➢ Influence with regulatory bodies and government departments.

By carefully considering the above factors and bringing regular improvements when possible will no doubt give the enterprise a competitive age as each factor can add to the ability of the enterprise to achieve its mission and objectives. It is important to note that with the advent of information technology it has now become possible to turn data and information into a potent strategic weapon. J. Hamiliton and C. L. Harris[7] have suggested ten ways to use information technology, namely: (I) better financial management, (ii) customer services, (iii) locking in customers, (iv) market intelligence, (v) new business, (vi) product development, (vii) sales, (viii) selling extra processing power, (ix) telemarketing, and (x) training. By implementing these suggestions the enterprise can develop strengths in gaining competitive advantage.

## 4.8 MARKETING AND DISTRIBUTION FACTORS

Marketing and distribution starts with finding out what customers want and whether the product and/or service can be sold at a reasonable profit. This area requires a care analysis of many activities such as

---

[7] Hamilto J. and C.L. Harris. "Information Power". Business Week, October 14. 1985, PP. 108-116

market research, identifying the market, developing product, testing product in the market from customers reaction, computing production costs, determining distribution and service requirements, and deciding on promotional approaches and advertising, etc. The following factors should be considered as a checklist.

> ➢ Cost effective and efficient market research system.
> ➢ Market share and competitive structure.
> ➢ Quality of products and services.
> ➢ Completeness of product-service line.
> ➢ Strong new product and new service leadership.
> ➢ Protection of patent rights.
> ➢ Customers/clients and consumers satisfaction.
> ➢ Efficient and cost effective packaging of products or deliverables.
> ➢ Cost effective and efficient marketing promotion activities (inc. advertising).
> ➢ Cost effective and efficient distribution channels.
> ➢ Cost effective and efficient after sale service.
> ➢ Cost effective and efficient sales force.
> ➢ Realistic pricing strategy for products and/or services.

By carefully considering the above factors and bringing regular improvements when possible will no doubt give the enterprise a competitive age as each factor can add to the ability of the enterprise to achieve its mission and objectives.

## 4.9   RESEARCH AND DEVELOPMENT AND ENGINEERING FACTORS

This function should not be dedicated to new entry but it can also provide significant strength for the ongoing business. This is a very important area which should be carefully analysed as it can be competitive advantage due to two primary reasons, namely: (a) it can lead to improves or new products, and (b) it can lead to the development of improved production or material process thereby providing cost advantages through increased efficiency which could be translated into improving pricing or margins. The following factors should be considered as a checklist.

> Basic research capabilities within the enterprise.
> Development capability for product engineering.
> Excellence in product design, process design and improvements.
> Superior packaging and capacity for further development.
> Improvements in use of materials (old and new).
> Ability to meet design goals and customer requirements.
> Adequately equipped laboratory and testing facilities.
> Experienced and well trained scientists, engineers and technicians.
> Suitable work environment for innovation and creativity.
> Competent management able to communicate effectively at all levels.
> Inherent ability to perform effective technological forecasting and projections.

By carefully considering the above factors and bringing regular improvements when possible will no doubt give the enterprise a competitive age as each factor can add to the ability of the enterprise to achieve its mission and objectives. Research and development process is commonly viewed as proceeding through the four stages, namely: (i) basic research, (ii) applied research, (iii) development research, and (iv) commercialisation.

## 4.10  FINANCE AND ACCOUNTING FACTORS

This is a very important area, which should be carefully analysed. The following factors should be considered as a checklist.

- ➢ Financial resources and strength (i.e. liquidity, leverage, cash flow, profitability).
- ➢ Effective capital structure and cost of capital.
- ➢ Effective financial planning, capital budgeting and working capital procedures.
- ➢ A sound inventory valuation policy.
- ➢ Efficient and effective accounting systems.
- ➢ Efficient and effective system for cost budgets and profit planning.
- ➢ Efficient and effective auditing procedures.
- ➢ Minimising risks by transferring risks when appropriate through insurance.
- ➢ Adequate investment of surplus capital.
- ➢ Amicable relation with stockholders and owners.

By carefully considering the above factors and bringing regular improvements when possible will no doubt give the enterprise a competitive age as each factor can add to the ability of the enterprise to achieve its mission and objectives. It is important to note that many entrepreneurs fail because they do not account for their financial weaknesses in their start-up phase.

## 4.11  ANALYSIS AND DIAGNOSIS OF THE GENERAL ENVIRONMENT

Environmental analysis is the process by which strategists monitor the environment sectors to find out opportunities for and threat to their enterprises, whereas environmental diagnosis consists of managerial decisions made from the assessment of the significance of the data of the environmental analysis with respect to opportunities and threats. The environmental analysis and diagnosis process is important for many reasons. Such as: (a) it helps in determining influence of environmental factors on strategy change, (b) it gives strategists time to anticipate opportunities and to plan to take optional responses to these opportunities, and (c) it helps strategists develop an early warning system to prevents threats or develop strategies which can turn a threat to the enterprise's advantage. Accordingly, in order to achieve corporate objectives, it is vital for the enterprise to adjust the environment to its strategy or react to the demands of the environment by changing its strategy.

The analysis's need to identify the current strategy the enterprise's uses to relate to environment and then search the environment to determine what factors in the environment present threats to the enterprise's strategy and objectives accomplishment and also to determine what factors in the environment present opportunities for accomplishment of objectives through an adjustment in the enterprise's strategy. The analysis should be done in such manners that it traces of an opportunity or threat to a source and involves breaking a whole into its parts to find its nature, function and relationship.

After consciously examining the relationship between the enterprise's strategy and their perception of the environment the strategists, by using acts of the analysis, identify the gaps (between the currents and future environment) and also form an opinion in order to determine the nature of a problem with a view to find out how best to take advantage of an opportunity or to effectively manage a threat. The strategist then make the assessment of the significance of the gaps to determine whether or not changes in objectives and/or strategy should be made, and the gaps should be reduced.

## 4.12  THE GENERAL ENVIRONMENTAL FACTORS

There are a large number of factors which affect the enterprise in each sector of the environment. For example for oil and gas industry such factors include:

- ➢ Government policy (i.e. safety legislation, pollution control regulations, etc.).
- ➢ Petroleum industry regulations (i.e.. market-share constraints).
- ➢ Economic and technological status (i.e. energy sources, materials sciences,
- ➢ vehicular sub-systems, electronics/communication systems, emission control).
- ➢ Competition (i.e. investment policy by competitor, regional strategy, range of services strategy by the competitors, etc.).
- ➢ Vehicle design configurations (i.e. power plant, fuelling system, support
- ➢ system, etc.).
- ➢ Personal vehicle servicing ( i.e. regional strategies with respect to servicing).
- ➢ Market structure (i.e. types of competitors and their market share by region).
- ➢ Credit systems (i.e. credit sales ratios by competitors, credit market share).
- ➢ Personnel expenditure distribution.
- ➢ Infrastructure configurations (i.e. dwelling-type distribution, vehicle ownership, By type of dwelling, commercial concentrations, etc.)

## 4.13 SOCIO-ECONOMIC, TECHNOLOGICAL AND GOVERNMENTAL FACTORS

There are many ways to organize the sectors for analysis and diagnosis such as socio-economic, technological and governmental.

### 4.13.1 Socio-economic Factors

For socio-economic sector the factors that should be considered may include but not limited to the following:

- ➢ **Economy** (i.e. the stage of business cycle – the economy is in a depression, recession, recovery or boom stage-, the inflationary or deflationary trend, monitory policies - interest rates, currency fluctuation -, fiscal policies - corporation and individual tax rate -, balance of payment – surpluses or deficits in relation to foreign trade. etc.). Each of the sub-factors of the economy can have an impact (help or hindrance) on the achievement of an enterprise's objectives and strategy may lead to success or failure of the business.
- ➢ **Climate** (i.e. climatic and ecological concern - unforeseen weather changes -, etc.). Ecological issues can affect plant location decisions and other related strategic decisions.
- ➢ **Society** (i.e. attitude of customers and employees, life style changes, etc). Social factor can affect strategy and may require keeping up with educational levels and social values, and making necessary changes in the strategies and policies by attempting to change social values and attitude through public relations efforts.

## 4.13.2 Technological Factors

The technological change can affect the enterprise's materials, operations, products, and services and can offer opportunities for improving goal achievement or threaten the existence of the enterprise. Pace of technological change is a function of innovation, creativity of people, deceptiveness on the part of industry availability of venture capital and risk taking, etc. However, not all sectors (some more volatile than others do) of the economy are likely to be equally affected by technological change.

## 4.13.3 Governmental Factors

National and local governments increasingly affect how enterprises operate by way of issuing laws and regulations. They issue legislation on such matters as: price controls; minimum wage; equal employment opportunity; health and safety at work; location of plant constraints; limit of chemical emission into the air; noise level; advertising constraints; and the way consumer credit is administered; etc.

Also government policies can affect the strategic choice of businesses. For example policies of large purchase of goods and service by the governments, subsidising to the industry by the governments, protection of home producers against unfair foreign competition by the governments, level of government spending on capital projects, and government policies that change economic conditions, tax laws, etc. The strategists must search the environment, devise the ways and means to influence government policies, and try to seize the opportunities and mitigate the threats that government policies may present.

Environmental analysis and diagnosis is a crucial part of strategic management process, therefore, top management must create the conditions that will facilitate effective analysis and diagnosis of the environment. If the environment is ignored or partially ignored by strategic decisions, the strategic management process will be less effective. Effective strategists always try to anticipate what is coming or attempt to influence the environment in favour of the strategic direction of their enterprises.

## 4.14 ANALYSIS AND DIAGNOSIS OF THE INDUSTRY AND INTERNATIONAL ENVIRONMENT

### 4.14.1 The Industry Environment Factors

An industry can be conceived of as a set of enterprises, which are in competition with one another for customers of their goods, and services and which rely upon others that supply critical inputs (i.e. suppliers). This implies that industry as a whole should be analysed and diagnosed in three sectors, namely customers, suppliers, and competitors.

### 4.14.2 Factors associated with Customer Sector

Effective strategists are concerned with who their customers are, where potential customers might be and what are their needs and desires, knowingly that opportunities come through identifying and providing for customer utilities and threat come from failure to meet changing customers requirements. The factors that should be considered for this sector include; (a) buyer identification, (b) demographic factors (i.e. changes in populations, age shift in the population, and income distribution of the population, etc), and (c) geographic factors (i.e. new location to add to current locations, area in which to relocate, moving out from city to a suburb or from one city to another, etc.).

### 4.14.3 Factors associated with Supplier Sector

Effective strategists are concerned with the cost and availability of raw materials, money, energy, subassemblies, etc. They are also concerned about supplier changes in the environment because suppliers provide capital, labor, material, and information to their enterprises thereby making them very important and powerful partners in the business operations. The factors to consider should include but not limited to the following:

➤ Availability and cost of raw materials and subassemblies.
➤ Availability and cost of energy (i.e. consider substitutes to remove the monopolies or fear of rising cost of energy from a single source).
➤ Availability and cost of money (i.e. awareness of the conditions in the money market and how they will affect strategy, etc.).
➤ Availability and cost of labor (i.e. relocating facilities in areas where specific skilled labor is available at a lower cost. Many major companies have a tendency to consider reallocating facilities in foreign countries to take advantage of lower-cost labor.
➤ Lead time (I.e. if supply of factors of production is not available when needed, the strategy may not be effective.

### 4.14.4 Factors associated with Competitor Sector

It is important to examine four factors regarding competition, namely: (a) entry of major competitors, (b) exit of major competitors, (c) substitutes and complements of current products and services, and (d) major strategic changes by current competitors. The are showed in Fig.2.5.

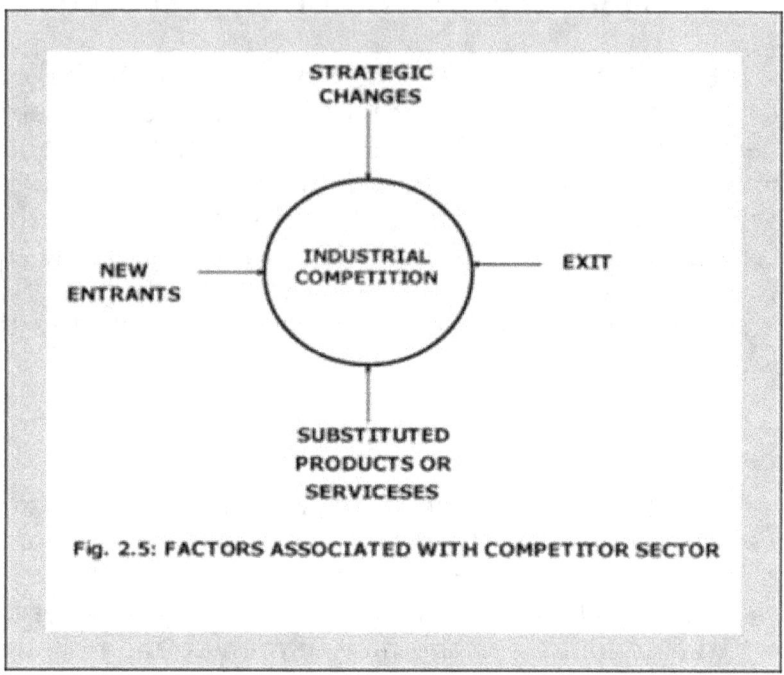

Fig. 2.5: FACTORS ASSOCIATED WITH COMPETITOR SECTOR

However, whilst analysing the competition strategic moves should be carefully watched to determine whether competitors are developing cost advantages, or taking market share or encroaching on market niches or developing new products, etc.

## 4.14.5 The International Environment Factors

He international environment is more competitive, complex, and heterogeneous and it must receive special attention from the strategists. For example relative values of currencies vary rapidly and can turn profits into losses in no time, and also inter-governmental and/or the enterprise to government relationships can have a significant bearing on the accomplishment of objectives.

Many opportunities for market or business expansion can be availed from international activities such as more favourable tax advantages, utilisation of cheap labour, chances of securing funding from international investors, benefit of global economy, etc. However, an international strategy can complicate an enterprise's structure and top executive relationships, which may in turn be able to bring threats to the enterprise.

Enterprises seeking to operate in foreign countries may face a variety of threats due to restriction placed on them by the host countries such as: ownership, employment, profits and fees, internal debt capital, host countries market, training and development, potential risks (i.e. political risks, social risks, economic risks, financial risks, etc), and technological basis, etc.

It is important consideration from the strategists to limit the analysis and diagnosis to the salient factors associated with their enterprises' activities as it is possible to do in-depth analyses and diagnosis of all the factor mentioned above and also to weigh all the pros and cons of threats which may offset the opportunities and advantages so envisaged.

# Chapter 5

## CHOICE OF APPROPRIATE STRATEGY

### 5.1 GENERIC STRATEGY ALTERNATIVES

In order to fill the gaps (after comparing the results of two profiles - e.g. expected and desired - and the enterprize's goals), the strategic decision makers generate alternative strategies. Relative to the gap analysis, the strategist starts from the current strategy. If identified gap is small or no gap at all, then the assumption, that current strategy is adequate thereby requiring little or no change, should be accepted. However, as the gap increases (identified by SWOT analysis or goal changes), then strategy alternatives to close the gaps should be considered.

Whether it is corporate level or business level strategy, there are four generic ways in which alternatives can be considered, namely; (a) stability, (b) expansion, (c) retrenchment, and (d) combinations of a, b, and c.

### 5.1.1 Stability Strategies

A stability strategy is a strategy that an enterprise pursues when it continues to serve the population in the same product or service, as defined in its business definition and also when its main strategic decisions focus on incremental improvement of functional performance. However, it should not be considered as 'do nothing' approach but instead should be considered as 'steady as it goes' approach (i.e.

keeping track on new developments and designing increase profits through improving efficiency in current operations and market share. However, this type of strategy is only effective when the enterprise is doing well and environment is not volatile.

## 5.1.2 Expansion Strategies

Expansion strategy is a strategy that an enterprise pursues when it serves the population in the additional product or service or adds markets or functions to its business definition and also when it focuses its strategic decisions on major increases in the pace of activity within its present business definition. An enterprise implements this strategy by redefining the business, i.e. by either adding to the scope of activity or substantially increasing the efforts of the current business. This strategy is often considered as an 'entrepreneurial strategy, when enterprises are found to develop and introduce new products or services or markets or penetrate market to build market share.

## 5.1.3 Retrenchment Strategies

Retrenchment strategy is a strategy that an enterprise pursues when it sees the desirability of or necessity for reducing its product or service lines, market or function and also when it focuses its strategic decisions on functional improvement through the reduction of activities in units with negative cash flows. This implies downsizing by using layoffs, reduced research & development, reduced marketing efforts or other outlays, and by increasing the collection of receivables, etc.

The retrenchment strategy is not so easy to pursue as it implies failure and it goes against the gain of most strategists. It is mainly reserved for dealing with crises and negative trends and to set the stage for more positive strategic alternatives and shift resources from loss making operations to innovation, new products or new markets.

### 5.1.4 Combination Strategies

Combination strategy is a strategy that an enterprise pursues when its main strategic decisions focus on the conscious use of several grand strategies (described above) simultaneously in various SBUs of the enterprize or to different future periods. This strategy is best for an enterprize whose divisions performs unevenly or do not have the same future potential.

### 5.2 STRATEGY VARIATIONS

Numerous variations of the generic strategy alternatives outlined above are possible for a given organization. Such variations for each strategic alternative are as follows:

**For Stability Strategy:** The strategy variations include internal, external related and passive. Internal variations may include seeking production and marketing efficiencies and reorganizationn. External variations may include maintaining market share. Related variations may include improving products or services or both. Passive variations may include reactive defence of position.

**For Expansion Strategy:** The strategy variations include: internal, external, related, unrelated, horizontal, vertical, active and passive. Internal variation may consist of penetrating existing markets, adding new products, or adding new markets. External variations may include acquisitions or mergers. Related variations may include seeking synergy from new products, new markets, or new functions (i.e. concentric diversification).

Unrelated variations may include conglomerating diversification in products, markets, or functions. Horizontal variations may include adding complementary products or markets. Vertical variations may include adding new locations. Active variations may include innovative or entrepreneurial moves. Passive variations may include imitating in research and development or new products.

**For Retrenchment Strategy:** The strategy variations include internal, external, related, unrelated, horizontal and vertical. The internal variations may include reducing costs, reducing assets, dropping products, dropping markets, or dropping functions. External factors include divesting SUBs, bankruptcies or liquidations. Related variations may include eliminating related products, markets or functions, Unrelated variations may include eliminating unrelated products, markets or functions. Horizontal variations may include eliminating complementary product or markets. Vertical variations may include reducing functions.

**For Combination Strategy:** The strategy variations include internal, external, active or international (sequential combination). Internal variations may include subcontracting some of the activities. External variations may include cross-licensing or entering into joint ventures. Active variations may include growing to sell out. The international variations may include seeking new international market for offensive or defensive reasons, introducing new products in foreign market for timing reasons or importing for domestic markets, setting up production units in foreign countries to take advantage of energy, resources, labor or technology available elsewhere at lower costs.

## 5.3. STRATEGIC CHOICE

Strategic choice is the decision to select from among the alternatives the strategy which will best meet the enterprise's objectives. The decision process involves focusing on few alternatives, considering the selection factors, evaluating the alternatives against these criteria, and making the actual choice. The alternatives should be chosen by trying to work forward from the present (where you are) to the future state (where you want to go) and devise the ways and means to get there (how to get there). Strategic choice is by and large influenced by four managerial selection, namely: (a) awareness of the past enterprise's strategies, (b) perception of external dependence, (c) attitude toward risk , and (d) power relationships.

Past strategies is the starting point of strategic choice and their awareness may element some strategic choices at the outset. For example, strategic change may be least likely if existing management group remains in power, it will be less likely if new executives are internally promoted, but is more likely when new managers are brought in from the outside.

The enterprizes do not exist in isolation from the external environment as they depend on other units (i.e. owners, competitors, customers, government, community, etc) for their prosperity and survival. The strategic choice will be less flexible if an enterprise is more dependent on the external units. It implies that the strategic choice is the outcome that is negotiated as various parties' manure to reach their objectives. It results from interactions of the enterprise with its environment.

The assessment of the manager's perception of risk will help the strategist to understand the potential acceptability of a given strategic option. For example, if risk is seen as necessary then stability can be eliminated as a possible option.

Power relationships are a key reality in organizational life and are major roadblock in making a correct strategic choice. For example, if the chief executive begins to advocate one alternatives, it may soon be unanimously accepted. The manager's personal goals, ambitions, values, and motivation can have a strong bearing on the choice of strategy. Therefore the strategist must analyse the values and goals of the key managers in order to determine the probability of acceptance of a given recommendation.

# Chapter 6

## IMPLEMENTATION OF SELECTED STRATEGY

### 6.1   STRUCTURE AND RESOURCES

Implementation is most important part of strategic management as even a well-worked out strategy is not likely to succeed without effective implementation. Also Implementation is necessary to spell out more precisely how the strategic choice will come to be. Fig. 2.6 is one consulting group (McKinsey & Company) presentation of the facts that strategy formation is but one component of a network of organization activities.

The McKinsey framework suggests that, to make a strategy to work effectively, the following components must fit together.

**Strategy:**   A coherent set of actions that an organization plans in response to or in anticipation of changes in its external environment, its customers, its competitors etc. with an aim to gain a sustainable advantage over competition (i.e. improve its competitive position in the market), improving position vis-à-vis customers, or allocation of resources.

**Structure:**_ The organization chart   (in which human being can perform most effectively) with accompanying baggage that show who report to whom and how tasks are both divided up and integrated (with individual responsibility and hierarchical distribution of authority).

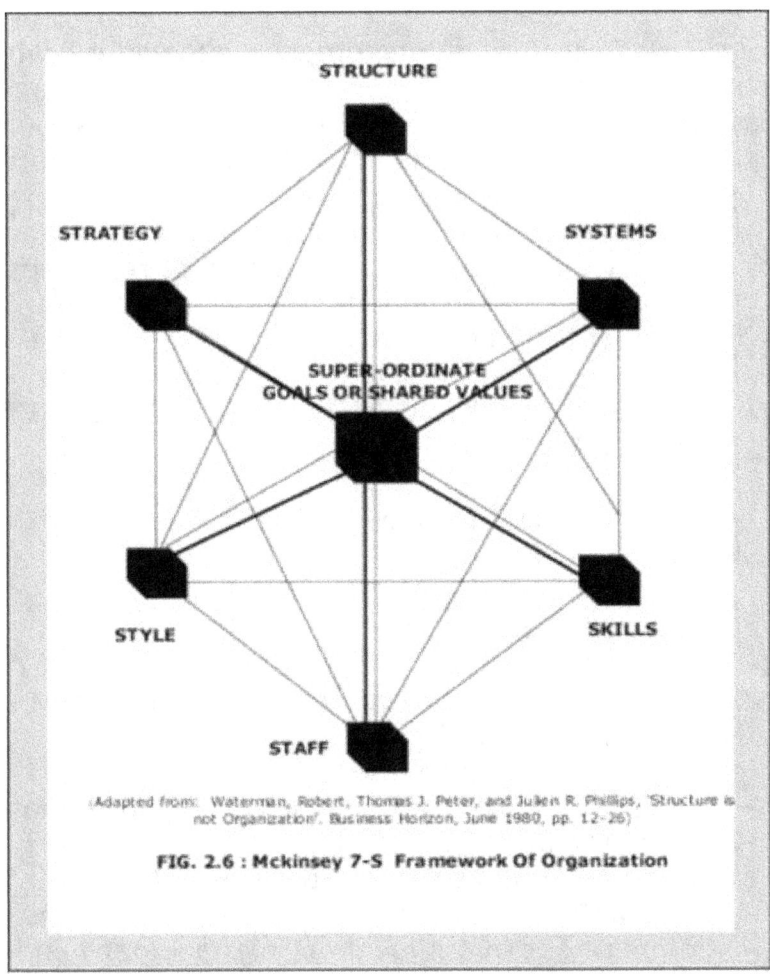

FIG. 2.6 : Mckinsey 7-S Framework Of Organization

**Systems:** Processes and work-flows that show how an organization perform routine operation e.g. information systems, production processes, QA/QC systems, performance measurement systems, and capital budgeting systems, etc.

**Skills:** capabilities that an organization posses as a whole as compared to the people in it.

**Staff:** The people (i.e. corporate demographics) in an organization

**Style:** It is management behaviour which provides tangible evidence of what management considers important by the way it (collectively as a unit) spends time and efforts and uses symbolic behaviour.

Implementation involves a number of interrelated choices and activities such as: allocation of resources of the enterprise, organisation design reflecting its strategy and objectives, etc.

## 6.2   THE FACTORS THAT INFLUENCE STARTEGY IMPLEMENTATION

The major factors include but not limited to the following:

> ➢ Strategy Formulation
> ➢ Executors
> ➢ Relationships among different departments and different strategy levels
> ➢ Adequate Communication Channels
> ➢ Consensus within and outside the organization
> ➢ Implementation Tactics
> ➢ Adequate Organisational Structure
> ➢ Organizational Administrative Control Systems
> ➢ Commitment by all levels of management and by employees

These factors are briefly discussed herein below:

### 6.2.1 Strategy Formulation

If the corporate strategy is vague or drafted by the business is a poor strategy, then it can dramatically limit the implementation efforts. According to Hrebiniak, good execution cannot overcome the shortcomings of a bad strategy or a poor strategic planning effort[8]. Several studies mention the fact that the kind of strategy that is developed[9] and the actual process of strategy formulation, namely, how a strategy is developed[10] will influence the effect of implementation. According to Allio, good implementation naturally starts with good strategic input: the soup is only as good as the ingredients[11]. Alexander believes that the need to start with a formulated strategy that involves a good idea or concept is the most crucial and critical factor which helps promoting its successful implementation[12].

## 6.2.2 Executors

Executors comprise the top management, middle management, lower management and staff function (non-management) advisers. According to Govindaraja, effectiveness of strategy implementation is, at least in part, affected by the quality of people involved in the process[13], here the quality refers to the capabilities, experience, skills, attitudes, and other characteristics of people required by a specific position[14]. Research

---

[8] Hrebiniak, L.G. (2006), "Obstacles to Effective Strategy Implementation". *Organizational Dynamics*, 35, 12-31.

[9] Alexander, L.D. (1985), "Successfully Implementing Strategic Decisions". *Long Range Planning*, 18, 91-97 and Allio, M.K. (2005), 'A Short, Practical Guide to Implementing Strategy". *Journal of Business Strategy*, 26, 12-21.

[10] Kim, W.C., and Mauborgne, R.A. (1993). „Making Global Strategies Work". *Sloan Management Review*, 34, 11-27; and Singh, D.T. (1998), 'Incorporating cognitive aids into decision support systems: the case of the strategy execution process', *Decision Support Systems,* 24, 145–163.

[11] Allio, M.K. (2005)., "A Short, Practical Guide to Implementing Strategy". *Journal of Business Strategy*, 26, 12-21.

[12] Alexander, L.D. (1985), 'Successfully Implementing Strategic Decisions". *Long Range Planning*, **18**, 91-97.

[13] Govindarajan, V. (1989), "Implementing Competitive Strategies at the Business Unit Level: Implications of Matching Managers to Strategies". *Strategic Management Journal*, 10, 251-269.

[14] Peng, W., and Litteljohn, D. (2001). „Organisational Communication and Strategy Implementation-A Primary Inquiry". *International Journal of*

findings of Hrebiniak and Snow indicate that strategy implementation effectiveness, critically depends on the human or people side of project management, and less on organization and systems related factors. Top management refers to the senior-level leaders including presidents, owners, and other high ranking executives (CEO, CFO, COO etc.) and senior-level managers. Hrebiniak and Snow report that the level of interaction and participation among the top management team typically leads to greater commitment to the firm's goals and strategies[15].

This, in turn ensures the successful implementation of the strategy. Gupta and Govindarajan noteed that greater the marketing and sales experience of middle managers, the greater would be their willingness to take risk and successfully implement the strategy[16]. It is important to understand that the lack of shared knowledge with lower-level management and non-management employees would create a barrier to successful strategy implementation. Heracleous fond that if middle management do not agree with the strategy, or do not feel that they have the skill set to implement it, then they would sabotage its implementation[17].

---

*Contemporary Hospitality*, **13**, 360-363.

[15] Hrebiniak, Lawrence G. and Snow, Charles C., "Decision-making-in-management; Organizational-effectiveness". *Human Relation (HR), 35, 1139-57*

[16] Gupta, A.K., and Govindarajan, V. (1984). „Business Unit Strategy, Managerial Characteristics and Business Unit Effectiveness at Strategy Implementation". *Academy of Management Journal*, **27**, 25-41.

[17] Loizos Heracleous is Professor of Strategy and Organization at the Warwick Business School and an Associate Fellow of Green Templeton College at Oxford University. He was previously Reader in Strategy at the Said Business School and an Official Fellow of Templeton College at Oxford. Prior to this he was Associate Professor of Business Policy at the National

Middle managers expect the direction from the top management but frequently feel that they are in a better position to start and evaluate alternative courses of action.

## 6.2.3 Relationships among different departments and different strategy levels

The fact that institutional relationships among different units/departments and different strategy levels play a major role in the outcome of strategy implementation, which has been stressed in many studies in the concerned field[18]. Walker & Ruekert noted that marketing policies, inter-functional structures and processes, corporate-business unit relationships and processes are a major influence on business strategy implementation. Implementation effectiveness is negatively affected by conflict and positively affected by interpersonal communication and not written.

Such interdepartmental dynamics are affected by senior management support informal integration and joint reward systems. Other relationships that have

---

University of Singapore, where he spent 7 years. He conducts research on strategic management from an organizational perspective, organization change and development, and organizational discourse. He has published many books (refer to bivliography)

[18] Walker, Jr, O.C., and Ruekert, R.W. (1987). „Marketing"s Role in The Implementation of Business Strategies: A Critical Review and Conceptual Framework". *Journal of Marketing,* **51**, 15-33; Gupta, A.K. (1987). „SBU Strategies, Corporate-SBU Relations, and SBU Effectiveness in Strategy Implementation". *Academy of Management Journal,* **30**, 477-500; Slater, S.F., and Olson, E.M. (2001). „Marketing"s Contribution to the Implementation of Business Strategy: An Empirical Analysis". *Strategic Management Journal.* **22**, 1055-1067; Chimhanzi, J. (2004, "The impact of marketing/HR interactions on marketing strategy implementation", *European Journal of Marketing,* **38**, 73-98 and Chimhanzi, J., and Morgan, R.E. (2005, "Explanations from the marketing/human resources dyad for marketing strategy implementation effectiveness in service firms". *Journal of Business Research,* **58**, 787– 796.

received attention to a lesser extent include finance, manufacturing, engineering, quality, marketing, accounting, and sales. In addition, allocation of resources, functional competencies, inter-functional conflict, decision-making participation and influence, and coordination also have different effects on the implementation of various kinds of business strategies.

## 6.2.4 Adequate Communication Channels

Communication includes explaining what new responsibilities, tasks, and duties need to be performed by the employees in order to implement the strategy. It answers the why behind the changed job activities, and explains the reasons why the new strategic decision was made. Many researchers have emphasized the importance of adequate communication channels for the process of strategy implementation, such as: Alexander (1985) noted that communication is mentioned more frequently than any other single item that promotes successful strategy implementation, and Rapert and Wren (1998) found that organizations where employees have easy access to management through open and supportive communication channels outperform those with more restrictive communication environments[19].

It is important to note that In communication is vital in every aspect of strategy implementation, as it relates in to the organizational context, organizing processes and the implementation objectives and effective communication is a fundamental requirement for any effective strategy implementation; whilst organizational

---

[19] Rapert, Molly Inhofe and Brent Wren (1998), "Reconsidering Organizational Structure: A Dual Perspective of Frameworks

communication plays an important role in training; and knowledge acquisition, and applied learning, during the process of implementation.

## 6.2.5 Implementation Tactics

Nutt stipulated four types of implementation tactics used by managers in making planned changes: intervention, participation, persuasion, and edict. Intervention refers to strategy adjustments made during the implementation stage by introducing new practices and norms[20], when participation includes formulating strategic goals and nominating a taskforce that can develop and propose the corresponding implementation options. Lehner considered the implementation tactics as genuine organizational behaviour based on the assumption that implementation in general is dependent on the environment, and various strategic and corporate variables[21]. On the other hand, persuasion is the tactic which uses involved parties to convince the employees about the desired course of actions and the issuing of directives is the main focus of the implementation tactic edict.

## 6.2.6 Consensus Within and Outside the Organization

Strategic consensus is the agreement between the top, middle, and lower-level managers on the fundamental policies of the organization. Strategic decisions are initiated by a team of top managers and then mandated to the rest of the organization, overlooking the importance of securing consensus with

---

[20] Nutt, P.C. (1986). „Tactics of Implementation". *Academy of Management Journal.* **29**, 230-261.

[21] Lehner, J. (2004). „Strategy Implementation Tactics as Response to Organizational, Strategic, and Environmental Imperatives". *Management Revue*, **15**, 460-480

and commitment to the organizational strategy with the lower level employees, which is a big barrier for effective strategy implementation. Nielsen (1983) noted that firms must achieve consensus both within and outside their organization in order to successfully implement business strategies, while the consensus about a firm's strategy may differ across the operation channels within the company.

If information passes through many layers in the organization, or if the employees of the company are not on the same information level, then a lower level of consensus would result and this lack of shared understanding may create obstacles to successful strategy implementation[22], whereas Floyd and Wooldridge label the gulf between strategies conceived by top management and awareness at lower levels as "implementation gap"[23].

## 6.2.7 Adequare Organisational Structure

If an organisation's realignment strategies are lacking, it may exhibit poor performance and be at a major competitive disadvantage. Drazin and Howard (1984); and Noble (1999b) stipulated that a proper alignment of the strategy with the organisational structure is an important pre-requisite for successful implementation of a corporate business strategy[24]. They noted that changes in the competitive environment

---

[22] Noble,C.H. (1999b). "The Eclectic Roots of Strategy Implementation Research". *Journal of Business Research,* 45, 119-134.

[23] Floyd, S.W., and Wooldridge, B. (1992b), "Middle Management Involvement in Strategy and Its Association with Strategic Type: A Research Note". *Strategic Management Journal,* **13**, 153-167)

[24] Noble,C.H. (1999b), "The Eclectic Roots of Strategy Implementation Research". *Journal of Business Research,* 45, 119-134.

require adjustments to the organizational structure. Accordingly, the type of strategy adopted could differ in many ways and have different requirements regarding an adequate organizational structure.

According to the study Heide & Grønhaug & Johannessen[25], factors relating to the organizational structure are the second most important implementation barrier.

## 6.2.8 Organizational Administrative Control Systems

The study of Roth, Schweiger & Morrison (1991) suggests that to create operational capabilities of configuration, managerial philosophy and coordination, to support business strategy implementation, organisational business units make use of three administrative mechanisms which are: formalization; integrating mechanisms; and centralization. Some researchers have also focused on the control systems which are one of important ingredients of administrative systems (Drazin & Howard, 1984; Nilsson & Rapp, 1999). Drazin and Howard (1984) discuss about the role of formal control system in the process of strategy implementation, and suggest that the fluidity of control system contribute to strategy implementation (Noble, 1999b).

## 6.2.9 Commitment by all levels of management and by employees

Strategy implementation process may fail if the strategy does not achieve support and commitment by

---

[25] Heide, M., Grønhaug, K., and Johannessen, S. (2002), "Exploring Barriers to The Successful Implementation of a Formulated strategy". Scandinavian Journal of Management, 18, 217-231.

the majority of employees and the middle management. Shared understanding without commitment would result in 'counter effort' and may negatively affect the organisational performance. The understanding between middle management and those at the operational level to that of the top management team's strategic goals is of prime importance to successful implementation. Noble & Mokwa (1999) have put forward three dimensions of commitment that are central factors which directly influence strategic outcomes: organizational commitment, strategy commitment and role commitment.

Organizational commitment is the extent to which a manager identifies with and works toward organization-related goals and values. Strategy commitment is the extent to which a manager comprehends and supports the goals and objectives of an implementation strategy. Role commitment is the extent to which a manager is determined to perform his individual implementation responsibilities, regardless of his personal beliefs about the overall strategy.

## 6.3  IMPLEMENTATION PROCESS

A proposed process of implementation of strategy is shown in Fig. 2.7.

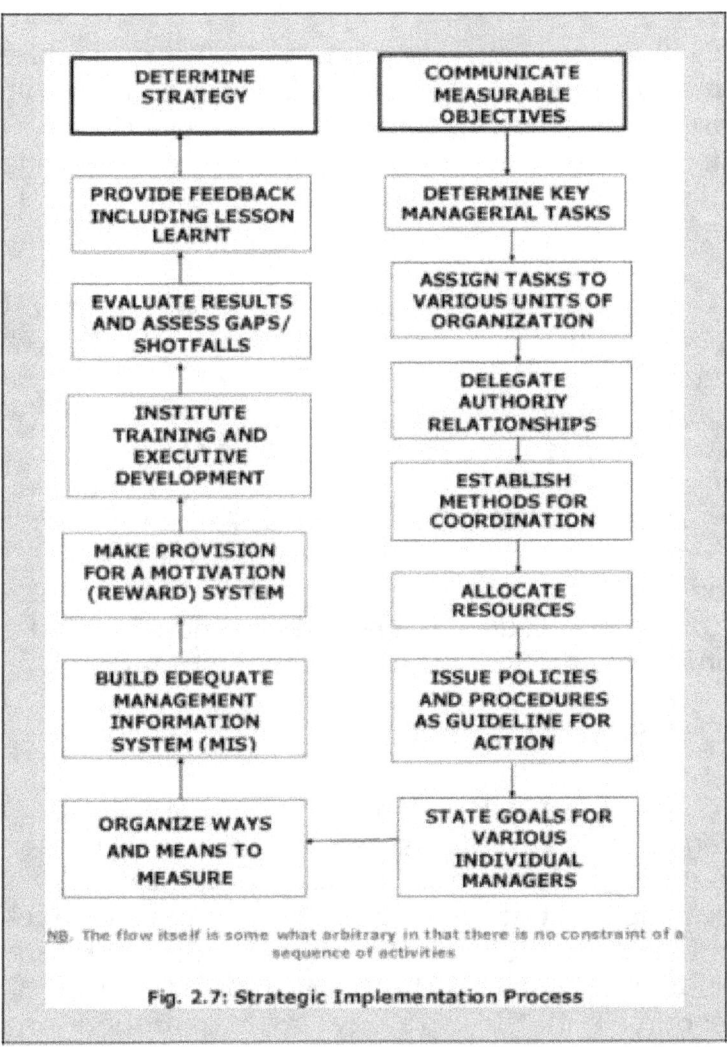

Fig. 2.7: Strategic Implementation Process

In the process of strategy implementation, various strategists play various roles. For example, corporate top managers decide on organizing and allocating of resources and making decisions on setting policies and administrative systems (with the help and advice of corporate planners and consultants). Likewise SBU top managers make above mentioned decisions for their respective units. Board of directors rarely involved in above-mentioned decision except when to approve major changes i.e. replacing a CEO or establishing different structures. Corporate planners and consultants act as advisors to the top managers in deciding where to allocate resources, how to organize, what policies to establish and how to co-ordinate and control the systems.

Once basic decision is made then their implementation is carried out through the basic structural hierarchy of the organization. At that point, any personnel or organization changes are made (which might be needed), tasks are assigned to the organization, budgets are provided, and communications (through the administrative system) are designed to inform employees of their responsibilities. However, for effective implementation, the process requires effective communication and negotiations among all the concerned strategists.

## 6.4    RESOURCES ALLOCATION

Resources allocation decisions are linked with strategies being implemented i.e. the development of competitive advantage. Critical organizational units (where the strategy is directed at creating competitive advantage) should, therefore, get preferential distribution of capital. The basic approach to allocation of resources in the strategy implementation process should be through the budgetary system because resources allocation (as expressed in the budget needs) need to be carefully linked to strategy. It is, therefore, important to understand various stages of budget process.    A typical framework for the strategic budgeting process in a large corporation with SUBs is shown in Fig. 2.8.

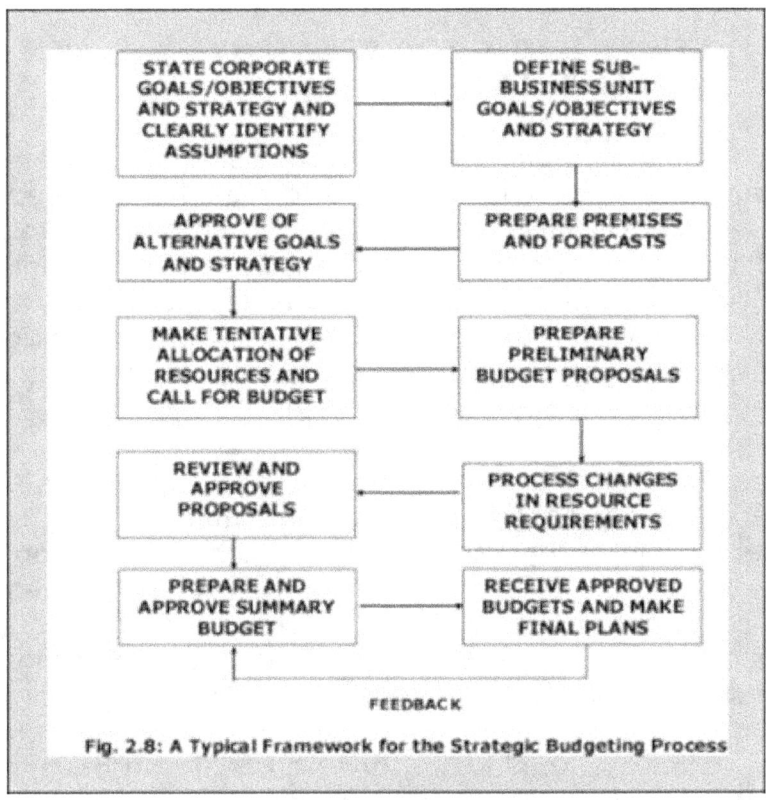

Fig. 2.8: A Typical Framework for the Strategic Budgeting Process

Step 4 (when top management examine the budgets and grant approval) is the stage at which the choice for allocation of resources is made i.e. who get the funds to recruit more personnel, buy new equipment or furniture, or build a new facility, etc.

It is important to note that due to the scarcity of resources not every units can be given what it wants, but nevertheless the top management must understand that if budget process is not tied up to the strategic direction of the enterprise, it can lead to problems. For example, loss of market fund at a strategic time can seriously affect a SBU's results.

## 6.5 STRUCTURING FOR STRATEGY IMPLEMENTATION

It is fundamental prerequisite of strategic management that the strategy and organization used by the enterprise must match. Since, organization involves dividing up the work among the groups and individuals (division of labor) and linking them in such a way that they will work together effectively (co-ordination), therefore, right organizational choice is a must for effective implementation of strategy.

In adopting basic structures for strategy, the strategists try to group duties and management sub-units in an optimum manner so that duplication of efforts and/or over specialisation is avoided. Since, strategy can rarely succeed without an appropriate organization therefore they should be determined simultaneously and must consciously linked together.

Many examples in the industrial world can be cited where well conceived strategic plans were thwarted by inappropriate organization structures that either delayed the execution of the plans or gave priority to the wrong set of considerations. Therefore, organization structure must evolve with changes in strategy and also must be the answer to the question 'which structure for which strategy' i.e. horizontal division of labor or departmentalisation (functional, product, customer, territorial, etc.) or matrix organization, etc.

## 6.6 PLANNING SYSTEM FOR STRATEGY IMPLEMENTATION

Planning (whether it is a function of the

mainstream of organizational life or of a dedicated planning department) is the key to effectiveness of strategy implementation process. Planners main task is twofold, namely to contribute to substantiate decisions about strategies and plans (content) and to set up the process in which substantive decisions are generated (i.e. instrumental role in the design and implementation of a planning system).

P. Lorange[26] opines that depending on the relative emphasis and tasks performed, planners might be viewed as catalysts (i.e. mostly involved in the process), analysts or strategists (i.e. mostly involved with content).

The catalyst roles include identify the need of the organization, developing a conceptual framework for planning tailed to the need so identified, co-ordinating with the line managers to discuss the system and also assisting them to implement the system in way of preparing planning manuals and reviewing of interdepartmental plans. The strategist (or analyst) roles include acquisition studies, identifying strategic options, narrowing down alternatives, providing information about choices and also advising on the relative merits of various proposals submitted by SBU executives, etc. However, the strategic roles of planning staff being crucial to strategy implementation process, have had a varying impact on the decisions whether to establish dedicated planning department or include the planning functions in the mainstream of organizational life. The following case study outlines this scenario.

For high impact strategic management it is more appropriate to split the strategic roles in such a way that the planning staff should perform analyses at

---

[26] Lorange, P..: "Corporate Planning: An Executive Viewpoint". Prentice-Hall, inc., Englewood Cliffs, N.J.

corporate level and the strategic decisions should be restored to those charged with the responsibilities of implementing the plans (i.e. line managers should play more significant roles in the content of strategic planning in the future).

The classic spilt between planners and line managers has prompted many companies in the past to reduce the planning staff and restore strategic decisions to those charged with implementing the plans i.e., mainstream of organizational life.

## 6.7    POLICIES, PLANS AND ADMINISTRATION

For an organization to implement strategy effectively, it requires some mechanisms to ensure that the activities are adequately integrated and co-ordinated, the plans developed are coupled with the strategies (to avoid any risk of plans moving the enterprise in an unintended direction) and obstacles encountered by the organization (through internal conditions) in implementing strategy are minimised.

This mechanism includes the development of plans, policies and administrative processes, which must be established to make a strategy to work. Plans and policies need to be developed to ensure that (a) the strategic direction is followed, (b) there is a adequate basis for control, (c) the amount of time executive spend in making decisions is reduced, (d) consistency in handling similar situations is maintained, and (e) where necessary, effective co-ordination across organizational units will occur.

For example, in order to find the answer to the question 'how do we get there, when and how' a manager has to prepare plans and corresponding policies to provide the means for carrying out plans and strategic decisions. However, to factor the grand strategy into plans and policies and to see that it is compatible and workable is not an easy task. It requires ability, appropriate competency and forward thinking.

## 6.8    PLANS AND POLICIES

For strategy implementation, plans and policies should (a) specify how the strategic choice will come to be (i.e. what is to be done, who is to do it, how it is to be done, and when it should be finished, etc). (b) Establish a follow-up mechanism to make sure the strategic choice, plans and policy decisions will take place, and (c) lead to new strengths which can be used for future strategy,

The processes involved in establishing plans and policies are quite similar to those, which influence formation of strategy, and choice as discussed above. Depending upon the nature, size, and operational complexity of an enterprise, plans and policies and be of many categories such as: (a) financial and accounting plans and policies (i.e. capital, lease or buy, risk assessment, use of assets, products & markets, distribution and promotion, price & packaging, etc.), (b) production-operation management plans and policies (i.e. location of facilities, capacity & utilisation, processes, equipment & maintenance, sourcing, etc.), (c) research and development plans and policies (i.e. basic & applied research, products and processes, offensive or defensive strategy, allocating research and development resources, etc.), (d) personnel plans and policies, (e) legal issues plans and policies, (f)  public relations plans and policies; etc.

A CASE STUDY

Wrap[27] described the following four ways in which companies organized for the planning function during the period when use of strategic planning was gaining impetus:

1. There was a planning committee composed of top management which was responsible for planning & operations; subcommittees undertook studies, whilst existing corporate staff groups were mad available on ad hoc basis.
2. There was a central planning committee with subcommittees to plan specific projects. The top management members assigned to the committee became full time planners with no operating responsibilities.
3. Planning was decentralised to a general manager in each division whist home office staff personnel were available for assistance on ad hoc basis.
4. A special planning unit was charged with responsibility for developing long range plans. However this approach created the classic split between planners and doers. The evidence indicated that line management seldom implemented completed plans.

## 6.9    INTEGRATING PLANS AND POLICIES

After all plans and policies, to aid the strategy implementation process, are developed by line and staff functions units the need to be integrated to ensure internal consistency in them and to see that key tasks needed to carry out a given strategy are accomplished. In variety of policy areas some trade-off decisions have to be made to to achieve optimisation in choosing

---

[27] Wrapp, E.: "Organization for Long Range Planning", Havard Business Review, Vol.35, no.1 (Jan.-Feb. 1957

alternative functional plans and policies. For example, for a business of high capital-intensive with high manufacturing cost, then a strong linkage and integration of plans and policies of research and development and manufacturing units will be helpful for developing cost-saving process improvements.

## 6.10 ROLE OF LEADERSHIP IN STRATEGY IMPLEMENTATION

In strategy implementation, providing appropriate leadership skill is a critical component of the administrative system. Leadership must be capable of helping organizations cope with change (when people may not necessary cooperate according to plans and procedures) and assuring that a follow-through of plans and policies occurs as planned. Effective leadership implementation can be achieved in several ways such as: (a) through making changes in current leadership at appropriate level, (b) initiating executive development training (i.e. developing appropriate leadership climate and styles), (c) using organization development techniques to effect changes, and (d) by initiating a program for career development for future strategists.

The important premises of leadership implementation include; (a) leader choice and assignment, (b) style & climate, (c) career development, and (d) organization development. However, effective leadership implementation involves ensuring that the person has acquired the right education, abilities, skills & experience, and possesses sufficient motivation and personality traits to enact the strategic choice.

## 6.11 STRATEGY IMPLEMENTATION IN INTERNATIONAL SETTINGS

The enterprise who wishes to pursue an

international strategy should explore issue associated with the special cases of (a) international resource allocation, (b) orgaization, (c) plans and policies, and (d) leadership implementation as discussed above.

## 6.12 EVALUATION AND CONTROL PROCESS

Evaluation and control processes help strategists monitor the progress of a strategic plan and seeking to find out whether or not (a) the decisions being made are consistent with the policy, (b) there are sufficient resources to get the job done, (c) the resources are being used wisely, (d) event in the environment are occurring as anticipated, (e) goals and targets are being met, and (f) the enterprise should proceed with the plan as it has been formulated. It implies that evaluation and control is that phase of the strategic management process in which management try to ensure that the strategic choice is properly implemented and is meeting the objectives of the enterprise and if gap between expected and desired objectives exists to ensure that it is closed according to the strategy.

In establishing the content of the evaluation and control system the major decision areas should include (a) the criteria for evaluation, (b) the tools to use in the control system, (c) feedback system, and (d) the outcome of the strategic evaluation.

The evaluation is thought of as a four interrelated activities as shown in Fig. 2.9. This process, however can encompass a variety of dimensions of importance to strategic management, such as: (a) management control (based on past performance and historic data), (b) real time control (which is concerned primarily with technical aspect of control), (c) performance management (which is concerned with goal congruence and organizational effectiveness), (d) adaptive control (concerned with determining the quickest and most effective way in which to respond to changes, and (e) strategic control (which involves anticipating or developing ways to minimise potential deviations) as Rowe and Carlson[28] pointed out.

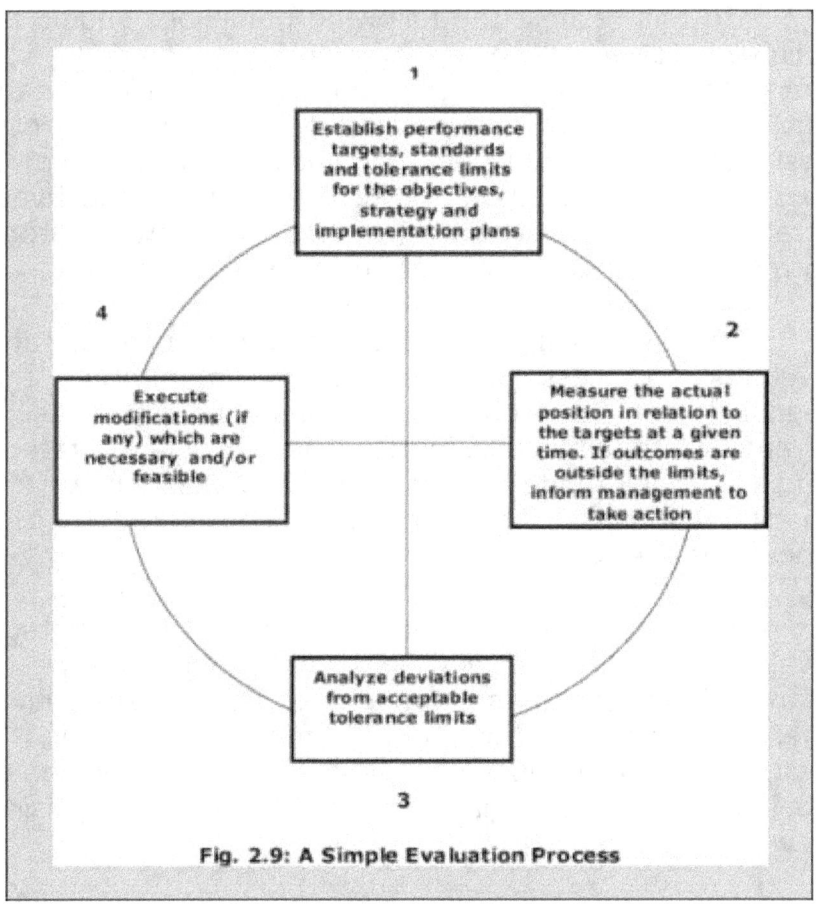

Fig. 2.9: A Simple Evaluation Process

The first two aspects (a and b) are mostly concerned with internal implementation questions, the third (c)

---

[28] Rowe, A.J., and J. Carlson: "Adaptive Control Systems for Operating Management", Logistic Spectrum Journal, September 1974.

involves question of objectives, whilst last two (d and e) are of more significance to questions of evaluating strategic validity and change. In order to effectively accomplish these types of controls, it is necessary to modify the process so that it also includes environment besides internal assessments.

In this respect the following guidelines should be followed: (a) establish environmental assumptions that are basic to the strategy and plans, (b) Monitor environmental factors  (related to the environmental assumotions) to detect any significant deviation, (c) If extraordinary deviation occur, reassess objectives, strategy and plans, and (d) execute new strategy formulation and implementation process accordingly.

This implies that the strategic control and evaluation process also require the monitoring and feedback of environmental conditions to ensure strategists that the assumptions on which the strategy and plans are made remain valid. Fig. 2.10 shows the modified process by taking into considerations the above requirements.

Stages 3 and 4 are where actual strategy evaluation is performed. If assumptions and or standards/tolerances are found below the desired level then appropriate adjustment is made. Conversely, if assumptions are found pessimistic, then the level of goals and objectives may be raised thereby recognising new opportunities.

It implies that during these stages, the strategists determine which of the cause-effect relationships are operating.

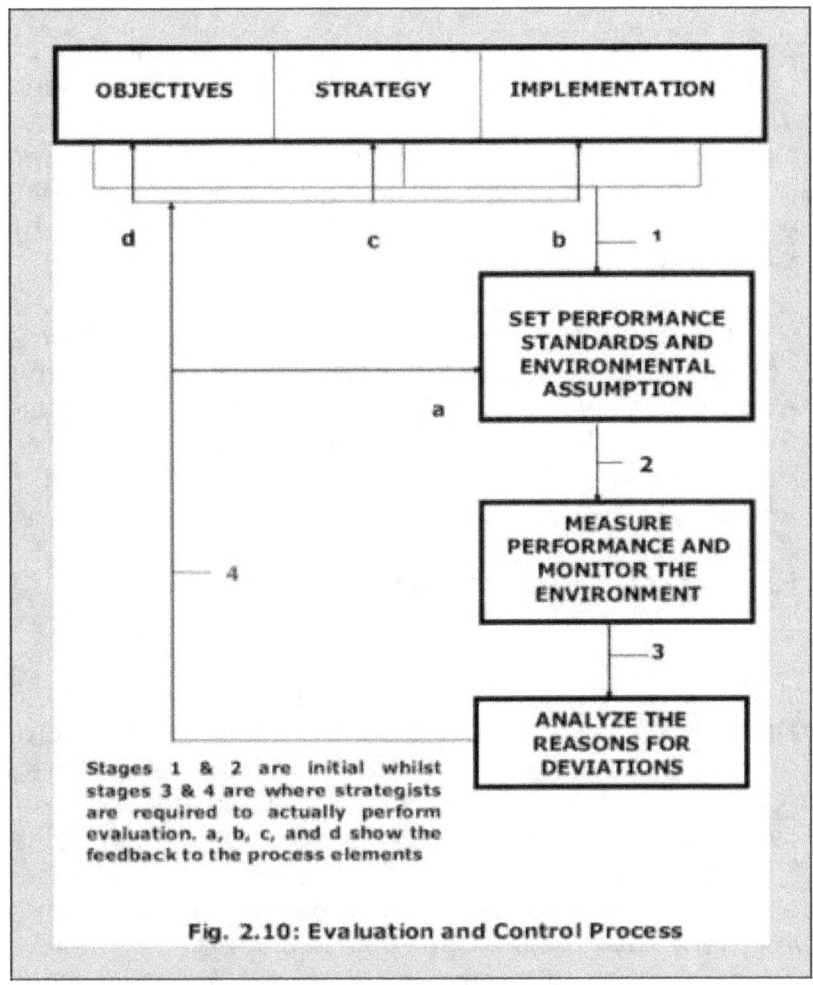

Fig. 2.10: Evaluation and Control Process

## 6.13 EFFECTIVENESS OF CONTROL AND EVALUATION SYSTEM

The motivation to evaluation by the top management is a key for effectiveness of the system and such motivation can only develop if senior managers realise that the strategy can fail which can affect their advancement (i.e. career development, promotion, salary rise, etc.) and also that they will be rewarded for effective performance in relation to the accomplishment of objectives. Although, by and large strategies must work but experiencing no failures can be dangerous because it may de-motivate the senior management to evaluate the strategies and business can fail due to lack of evaluation. It implies that some failures are healthy as they remind the management to determine whether the strategies are effective (i.e. they are working).

The inducement and reward system will have a major impact on the effectiveness of evaluation system. The managers will be motivated to evaluate strategies more effectively if they know that their high performance in relation to meeting objectives will be rewarded.

## 6.14 CRITERIA FOR EVALUATION

Due to the complexity of the field of organizational effectiveness (i.e. defining and measuring evaluation factors), it is not easy to choose the factors upon which to focus the evaluation. To overcome this difficulty, multiple criteria should be used as single criterion may lead to non-optimal or undesirable results. For example, short-term profitability is not by itself an adequate measure of managerial performance return on investment by itself may lead to postponement of needed research or upgrading equipment and facilities, and so on. However, selection of a set of criteria depends to a large extent on the nature and purpose of evaluation. In this respect Christenssen[29] opines in the following words:

'The management evaluation system, which plays so great a part in influencing management

---

[29] Christensen, C. R., K. R. Andrews and L. J. Bower: "Busuness Policy: Text and Cases", Homewood, Ill, Irwin, 1978, p. 644.

*performance, must employ a number of criteria, some of which are subjective and thus difficult to quantify. It is easy to argue that subjective judgements are unfair. But use of harmful or irrelevant criterion just because it leads itself to quantification is a poor exchange for alleged for objectivity.'*

In selecting the criteria a happy medium should be adopted between quantitative measurement and subjective judgements (on areas such as: consistency, appropriateness, and workability, etc.).

## 6.15 PERFORMANCE MEASUREMENT AND FEEDBACK

The timing when results should be evaluated is a most crucial factor of the performance and control system. For example, if standards are set to be achieved in say 3 years and measurement does not take place until the end of third year, it may be too late to take remedial action to correct deviations and also to take advantage of opportunities which may pass by, and if it is made too early it may have knee-jerk reaction which could prevent the plan from having chance to work and also it is often difficult to change strategic direction quickly, particularly for large and complex organizations.

It is, therefore, appropriate for the top management to specify the timing for expected or desired results and provide benchmarks for progress. However, when a significant or critical deviation (negative or positive) from the planned assumptions or outcomes is identified, then the top management must be altered immediately. To make the process of performance measurement more effective the following course of action is suggested.

'The management should establish the critical success factors as major milestone on a critical path method (CPM) network. Long-term targets should be broken down into sub-factors for intermediate accomplishments Assumptions about the cause-effect relationships should be proceeded in the means-end chain. Then periodic measurements can be effected to make a comparison of intermediate progress with the intermediate planned accomplishments (or milestone on the CPM network). Depending on the variables, such periodic measurements may be taken quarterly, half yearly or annually".

The flow of information (usable and timely), particularly with respect to feedback, is crucial for the managers who have discretionary authority to make decisions about the critical success factors. These demands: (a) an honest and complete reporting of results of the strategy, and (b) an effective management information system (MIS). The enterprise should, therefore not only adopt an effective MIS but also encourage complete and accurate reporting so that top management can react to reversals and reinforce progress.

## 6.16 TOOL FOR FEEDBACK AND EVALUATION

MIS is a major tool for feedback and evaluation, and it can be a crucial factor in the implementation of strategy in an enterprise. It must be set up to provide the right information to the right people at the right time and should be designed in such a way that it can be used to help in effectively controlling the enterprise's outputs. Bertram Colbert define MIS as follows:

*"A management information system, simply, is an organized method of providing each manager with all the data and only those ideas which are needed for decision, when they are needed, and in a form which aids understanding and stimulates action"[30].*

MIS has also been defined as a system of obtaining, abstracting, storing, retrieving and applying data (new facts) to produce information for managers, at the time when they can most effectively use it. Whatever, the definition we may adopt, it is clear that MIS reduces uncertainty in decision making and optimises the value of information/intelligence within the organization structure itself.

MIS may be broken down into three levels namely: (a) reflex actions or routine operations (operations & lower management), (b) tasks involving well defined thinking (middle management), and (c) tasks involving creative thinking and strategic planning. MIS application relevant to those 3 levels is shown in Fig. 2.11.

Management functions, by and large, can be grouped under two major phases namely: Planning Phase and Control Phase, which in turn are very strongly interrelated. Therefore, MIS is not only a useful tool of managerial control, but equally so for other functions. For example, new enterprises start with the planning phase, i.e. forecast which leads to planning and then organization (to implement the plan); followed by the control phase. During control phase the functional (or action) processes are required to be executed by utilisation of men, machines and material through the

---

[30] Colbert, Bertram. -*The Management Information System'/* Management Services, Sept.-Oct. 1967, pp. 15-24.

managerial functions of commanding (or directing), co-ordinating and control.

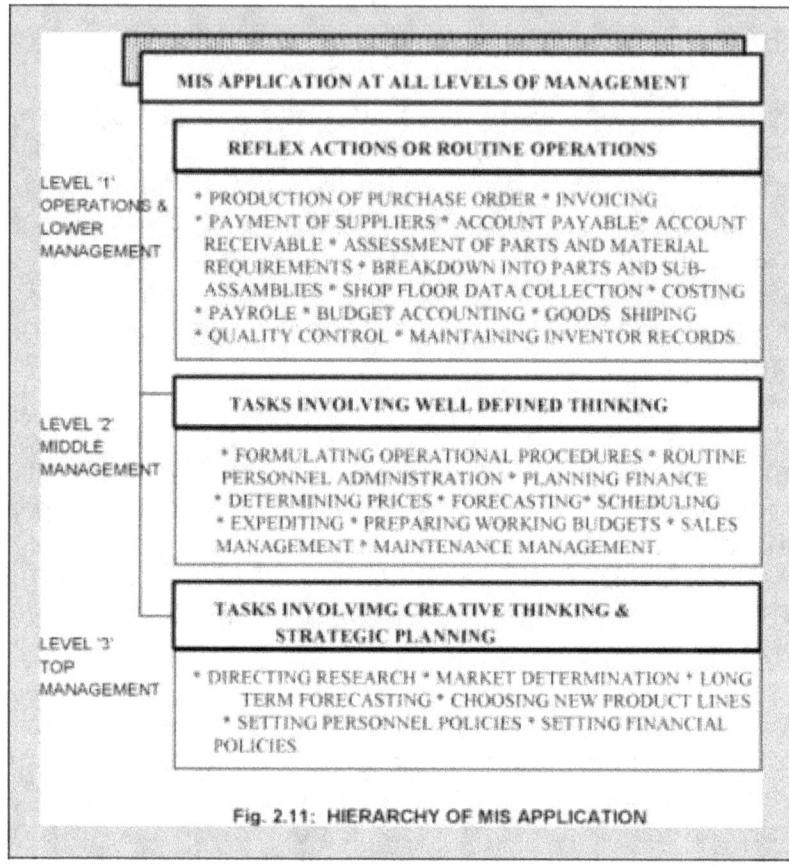

**LEVEL '1'**
**OPERATIONS &**
**LOWER**
**MANAGEMENT**

**LEVEL '2'**
**MIDDLE**
**MANAGEMENT**

**LEVEL '3'**
**TOP**
**MANAGEMENT**

**MIS APPLICATION AT ALL LEVELS OF MANAGEMENT**

**REFLEX ACTIONS OR ROUTINE OPERATIONS**

* PRODUCTION OF PURCHASE ORDER * INVOICING * PAYMENT OF SUPPLIERS * ACCOUNT PAYABLE* ACCOUNT RECEIVABLE * ASSESSMENT OF PARTS AND MATERIAL REQUIREMENTS * BREAKDOWN INTO PARTS AND SUB-ASSAMBLIES * SHOP FLOOR DATA COLLECTION * COSTING * PAYROLE * BUDGET ACCOUNTING * GOODS SHIPING * QUALITY CONTROL * MAINTAINING INVENTOR RECORDS

**TASKS INVOLVING WELL DEFINED THINKING**

* FORMULATING OPERATIONAL PROCEDURES * ROUTINE PERSONNEL ADMINISTRATION * PLANNING FINANCE * DETERMINING PRICES * FORECASTING* SCHEDULING * EXPEDITING * PREPARING WORKING BUDGETS * SALES MANAGEMENT * MAINTENANCE MANAGEMENT.

**TASKS INVOLVIMG CREATIVE THINKING & STRATEGIC PLANNING**

* DIRECTING RESEARCH * MARKET DETERMINATION * LONG TERM FORECASTING * CHOOSING NEW PRODUCT LINES * SETTING PERSONNEL POLICIES * SETTING FINANCIAL POLICIES

**Fig. 2.11: HIERARCHY OF MIS APPLICATION**

This two phased process of management functions is shown in Fig. 2.12. Since all management functions depend upon information, therefore, a good MIS is a key to managerial effectiveness.

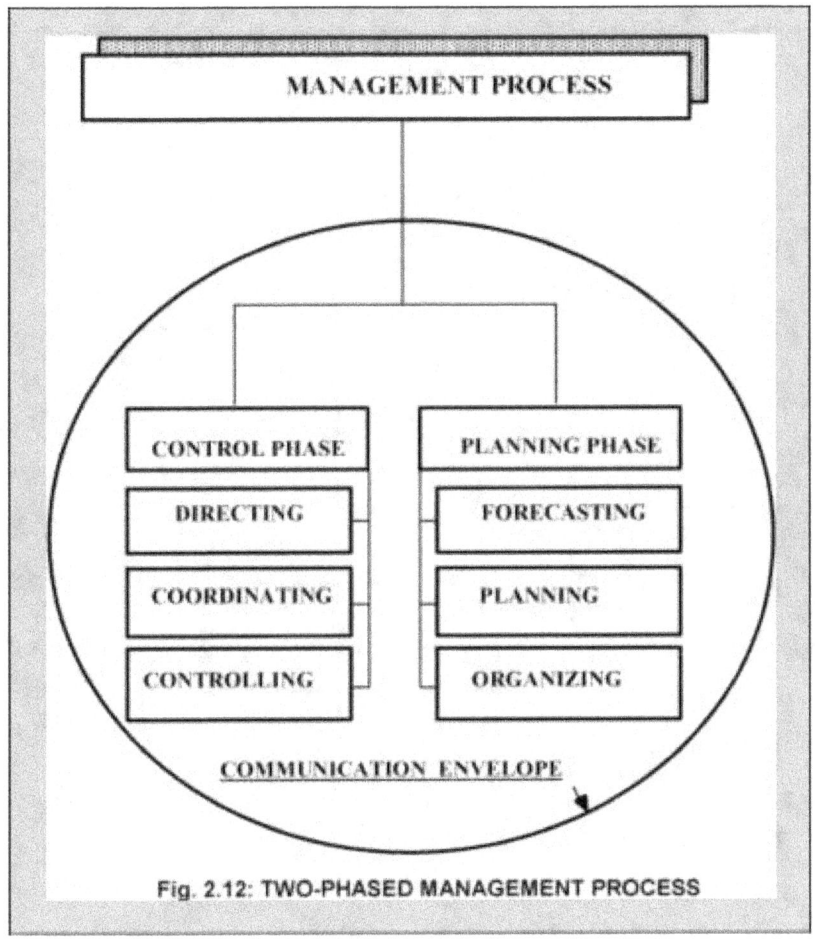

Fig. 2.12: TWO-PHASED MANAGEMENT PROCESS

MIS in action is shown in Fig. 2.13.

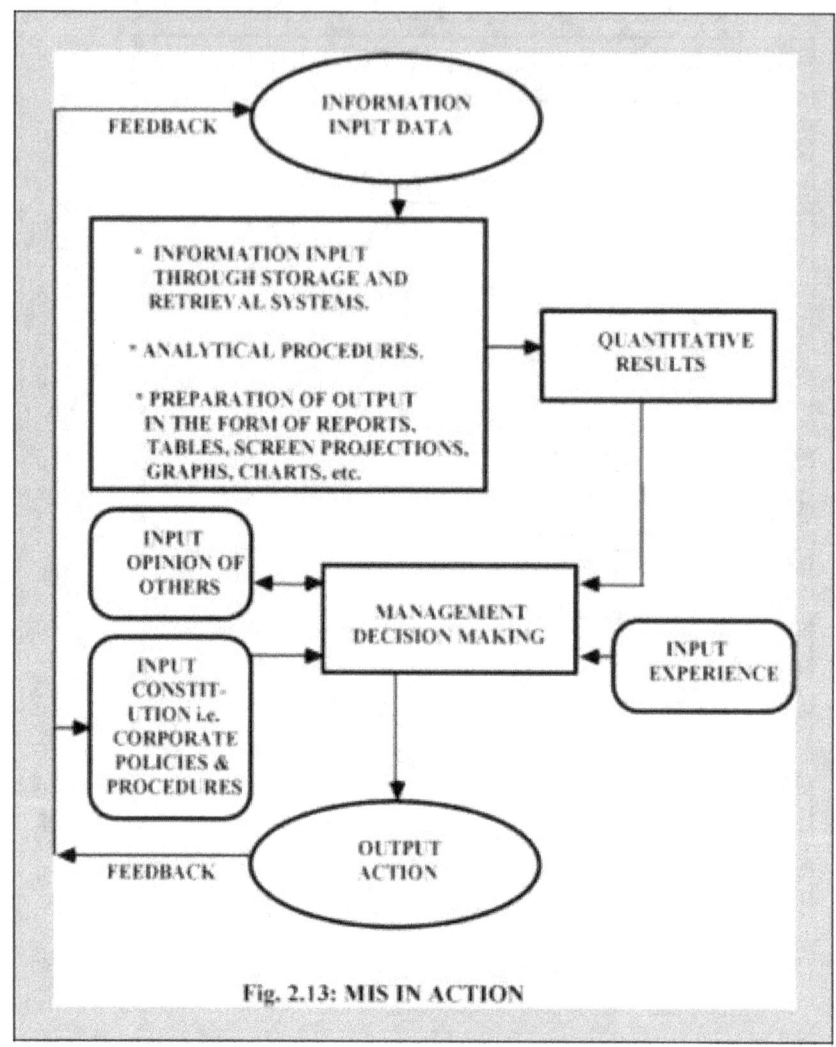

Fig. 2.13: MIS IN ACTION

## 6.17    MANAGEMENT BY OBJECTIVES (MBO)

MBO system in its idealistic form is a management tool which can help managers to accomplish the prescription as outlined above by combining of objective setting, planning, control, and reward systems, all of which are so crucial to effective strategy formulation and its implementation.

Management By Objectives (MBO) is a style of management of an organization, which emphasises the achievement of results expressed in terms of objective. In MBO process both supervisor and subordinate jointly set overall organizational goals and define each individual's area of responsibility in terms of the expected results. These measures are then used as guidelines for operating the respective organizational unit and also performance appraisal of its members.

However, there is a strong constraint attached to the MBO process that objectives must be specific, time bound, realistic, quantitative, qualitative and measurable. In essence, MBO emphasis the importance of subordinates' setting specific objectives, with the help and concurrence of their supervisors that are intended to be achieved within the period mutually decided upon, and then having their performance measured against the pre-set objectives.

Research of Robert H. Mills in an engineering & research environment, has identified that a direct relationship existed between experiencing ambiguity and job tension, personal ineffectiveness, job dissatisfaction and unfavourable attitude towards work associates; and suggest that to reduce these industrial ailments, a program of MBO would be appropriate[31]. Because MBO is based on better communication, co-operation and participation by all levels in the organization, it can realise benefits to all organizational participants. This is

---

[31] Mills, Robert H.- 'How Job Conflict and Ambiguity Affect R & D Professionals'/ Research Management, Vol. XVIII, No. 4, July 1975.

why both managers and subordinates often welcome it alike.

MBO is behavioural approach to management in which emphasis is placed more on relationships, than positions and information flow is both ways (unlike conventional approach in which information flow is priority downward and emphasis is on positions rather than relationships). Therefore, MBO approach provides a better co-ordination among various organizational units and leads to better understanding between the superiors and the subordinates. There are six elements of 'MBO' Process which may be considered critical to the successful implementation of 'MBO'. The process is shown in Fig. 2.14.

The process starts with good preparation including orientation to all members of the management team with an emphasis that active involvement in the 'MBO' program is an integral part of each manager's job.

The next step is to communicate organization goals (including the CEO directive) to subordinates at each level of organization hierarchy and review/discuss the superior's important job responsibilities, followed by the discussion and joint agreement on key effectiveness of components of subordinate's job.

Once understanding is built up regarding responsibilities and obligations of both superior and subordinates, next step is to jointly set objective, targets and performance criteria followed by interim progress review and finally evaluating performance and distribution rewards with a feedback to the process for further developed.

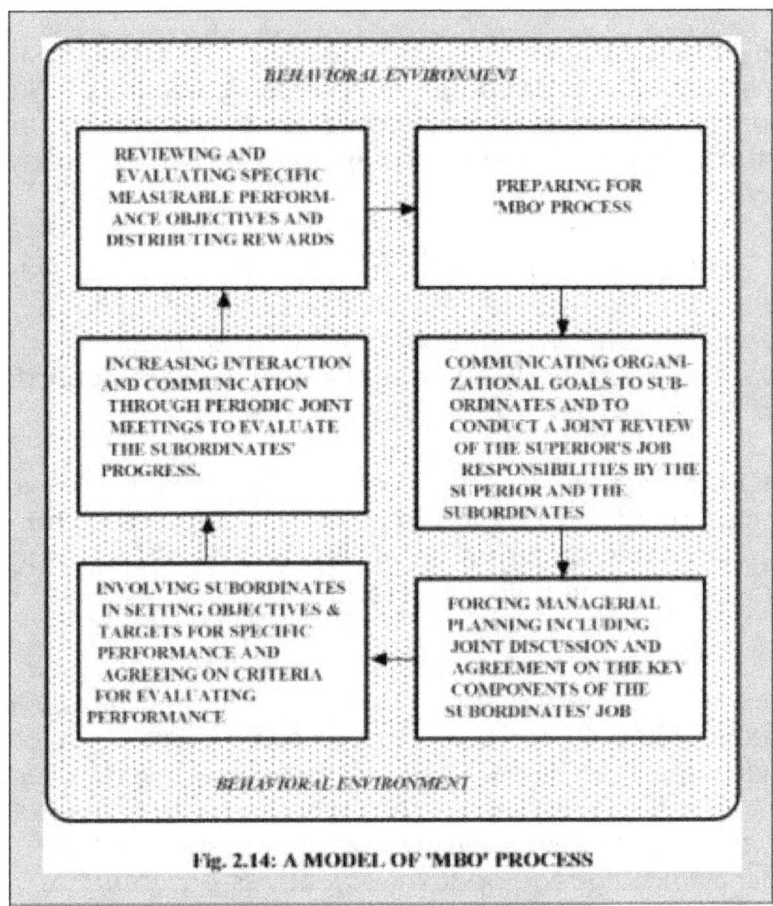

Fig. 2.14: A MODEL OF 'MBO' PROCESS

Although MBO holds great promise as a powerful management tool, in impressing managerial effectiveness but nevertheless in actual practice it is vested with numerous pitfalls and shortcomings, resulting in a number of managers holding a negative view towards its implementations. Therefore, for each manager there is a challenge to build on the strength of MBO and or overcome its pitfalls. To achieve these twofold goals, managers should follow the guidelines suggested by Harold Koontz in his book: 'Shortcomings and Pitfalls in Managing by objectives'[32]. Emphasising a conscientious application of these guidelines, Harold Koontz advocates the importance of MBO as a comprehensive system of management in the following words.

*"Management by objectives must be a way of managing, a way of planning as well as the key to organizing, staffing, directing, and controlling - it is then a part of managing, a summary of what has been done, and not a difficult separate operation"[33].*

MBO, though it can be a ver useful tool for effective management, but it is not a panacea for all organizational ailments as Martin and Shell quite rightly expressed in the following worlds.

*"Management by objectives is not a panacea, but it can be a very useful tool in improving managerial effectiveness in the engineering and scientific environment. While it is not easily applied, there is considerable evidence to suggest that technical organizations can benefit from a well-planned and functioning management by objectives program"[34].*

## 6.18    EVALUATION AND CORRECTIVE ACTION

The final phase of evaluation and control is the use of timely information to reward performance which

---

[32] Koontz, Harold.- '*Shortcomings and Pitfall in Managing by Objectives*'/ Management By Objectives, Jan. 1972, pp.6-12.

[33] Koontz, Harold.- '*Making Managerial Appraisal Effective*'/ California Management Review, Vol. 15, No. 2, Winter 1972, p. 51.

[34] Martin, Desmond D. and Richard L. Shell.- 'What Every Engineer should know about Human Resources Management'/ New York: Marcel Dekker, Inc. p. 156

remains in control or to determine the causes of deviations and take corrective action. The evaluation (after-the-fact) and corrective actions should be proceeded as outlined in Fig. 2.10 above. Stage I poses the question 'are the performance standards too low or too high or are the environmental assumptions justifiable'. If answer is yes the performance standards can be readjusted, but if answer is no then stage 2 to be activated. Stage 2 poses the question 'is the implementation inadequate or are policies, resources or organization changes needed'.

If answer is yes, make necessary alterations, but if answer is no then activate state 3. Stage 3 poses the question 'is the strategy inadequate or has the environment changed unexpectedly or is the contingency plan needed'. If answer is yes, use the contingency plan or begin to formulate a new strategy, but if the answer is no, activate stage 4. Likewise stage 4 poses the question ' how can we alter our objectives or convince others that the gaps in performance are within acceptable limit'. Answer to this question means providing an honest and accurate feedback. The top management should use the timely information to determine the cause of deviations and take corrective actions in closing the gaps and appropriate reward performance when objectives are accomplished as envisaged.

## 6.19 SUCCESSFUL MANAGEMENT IN TODAY'S ELECTRONIC AGE

In today's electronic age, the corporate joints particularly the electronic elite (e.g. Microsoft, Hewlett-Packard, Campaq, Dell Computer, etc.) has revolutionised the way business is done today. They have not only flattened corporate pyramids and redrawn communication channels but also proved that traditional hierarchies (which worked well during the industrial revolution) are not suited today when employees at all levels have ready access to huge storehouse of information.

They do not see the business as a battlefield but instead they see the business as an ecosystem. They view the corporation as a community not a machine, with a firm belief that role of management is not to just control but also to serve. They do not treat their employees as children but instead treat them as peers.

They motivate and inspire their workforce not through fear but through vision so that change is embraced as an opportunity and source for growth rather than a threat and source of pain. Therefore, in this electronic age, it has become vital for the organizational researchers to consider rebuilding the strategy by bringing new corporate culture in the business world.

Geoffrey James has proposed thirty-four strategies for successful business in his book "Business Wisdom of the Electronic Elite" published by Time Business, Random House, Inc, NY. The author has adapted these in the following models. A Framework of successful management in today's electronic age is shown in Fig. 2.15.

Whereas the corresponding strategies for each element are shown in Figs. 2.16, 17, 18, 19, 20, 21 and 22.

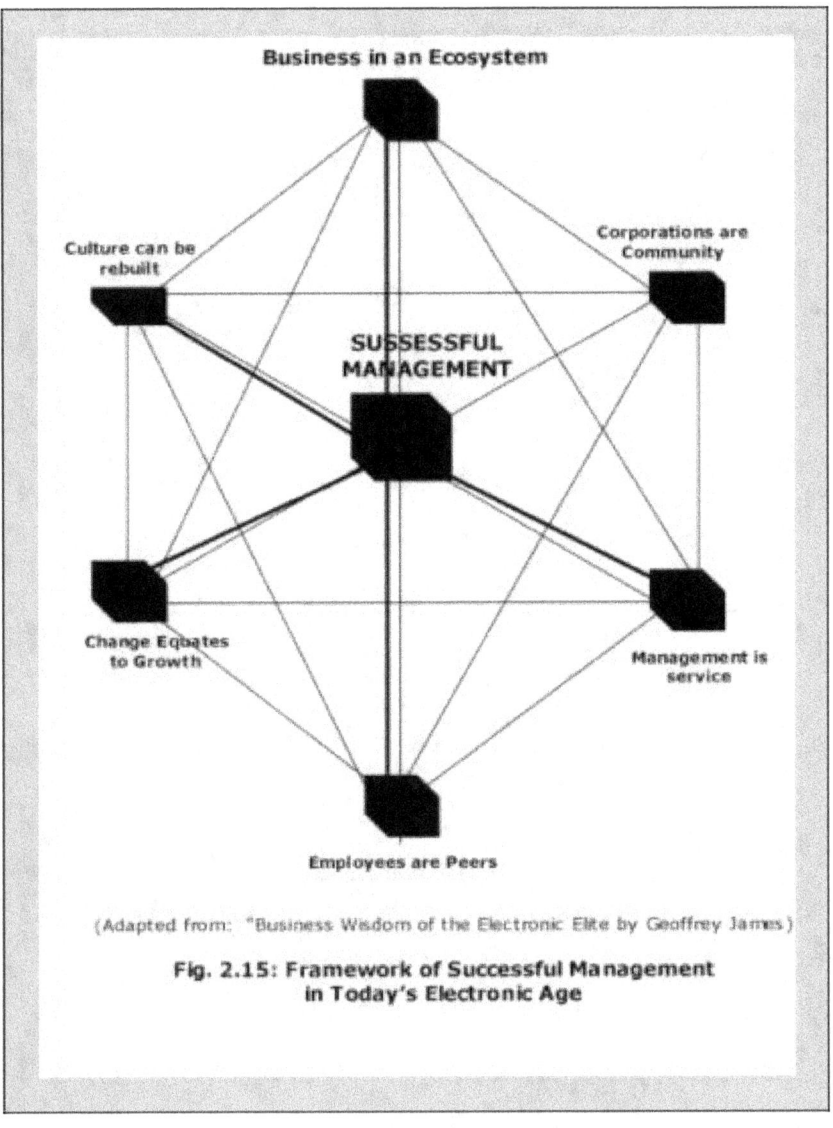

(Adapted from: "Business Wisdom of the Electronic Elite by Geoffrey James)

**Fig. 2.15: Framework of Successful Management
in Today's Electronic Age**

# Role of Strategic Management in Business Organizations

**VIEW BUSINESS AS AN ECOSYSTEM**

**Stg. 1**

**ENCOURAGE DIVERSITY**
Participate in different businesses with a variety of different models. Hire talented people with experience of different backgrounds who can contribute to create a more adaptive corporate culture

**Stg. 2**

**LAUNCH NEW GENERATIONS OF PRODUCTS**
It is not wise to wait for competitors to replace your product which is dying. Start now and think growing the next generation of product.

**Stg. 3**

**BUILD SYMBIOTIC (SYNERGETIC) RELATIONSHIPS**
Seek co-operation even with your competitors with a view to increase business of all co-operating companies.

**Fig. 2.16: Strategies for Viewing Business as an Ecosystem**

**VIEW CORPORATIONS AS COMMUNITIES**

**Stg. 4**

**COMMUNICATE DIRECTLY**
To exchange information about shared goals and responsibilities, no doubt encourages a sense of community. Accordingly, it is important to keep all employees at all levels of the company connected by every available forum.

**Stg. 5**

**CREATE OPPORTUNITIES FOR SOCIAL INTERACTION**
Employees should not be locked in the offices but must be given chances to get them together outsides the offices from time to time and encouraging them to participate in meetings and other events for social interactions.

**Stg. 6**

**MAKE WORK FUN**
It is important and logical to make work fun so that the employees can enjoy their jobs and work harder and longer due to labor of love.

**Fig. 2.17: Strategies for Viewing Corporations as Communities**

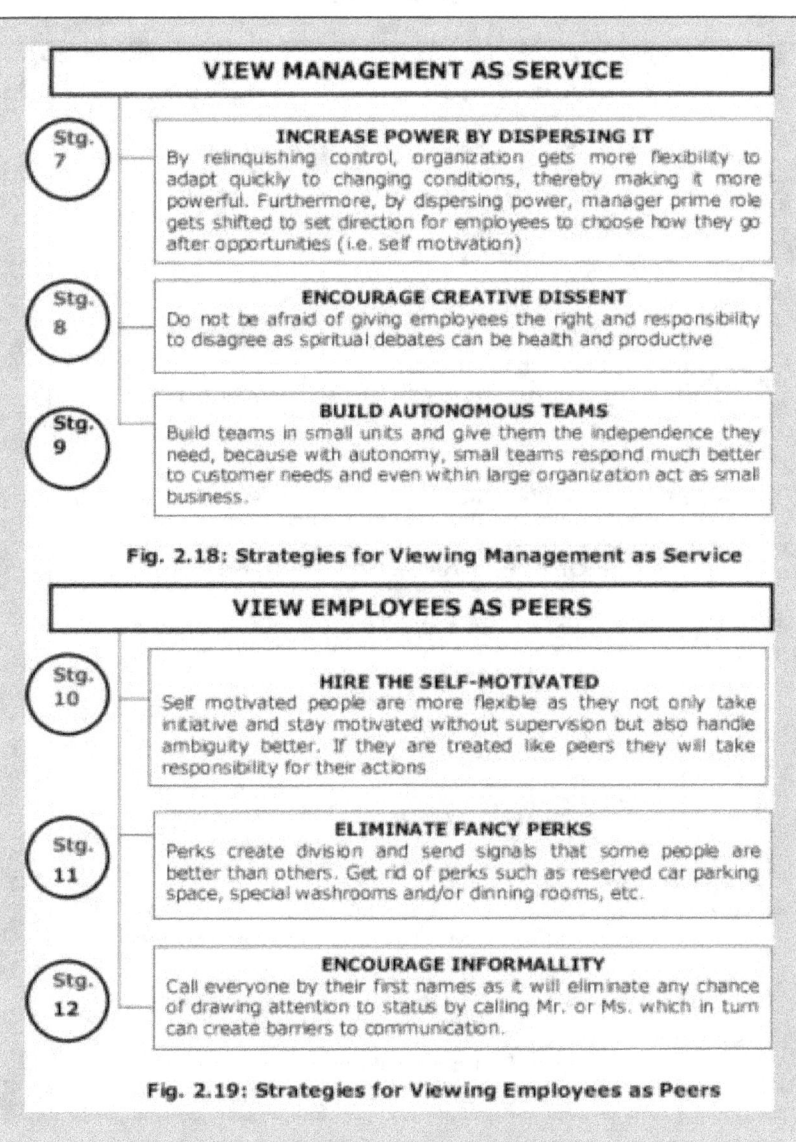

**VIEW MANAGEMENT AS SERVICE**

Stg. 7

**INCREASE POWER BY DISPERSING IT**
By relinquishing control, organization gets more flexibility to adapt quickly to changing conditions, thereby making it more powerful. Furthermore, by dispersing power, manager prime role gets shifted to set direction for employees to choose how they go after opportunities (i.e. self motivation)

Stg. 8

**ENCOURAGE CREATIVE DISSENT**
Do not be afraid of giving employees the right and responsibility to disagree as spiritual debates can be health and productive

Stg. 9

**BUILD AUTONOMOUS TEAMS**
Build teams in small units and give them the independence they need, because with autonomy, small teams respond much better to customer needs and even within large organization act as small business.

**Fig. 2.18: Strategies for Viewing Management as Service**

**VIEW EMPLOYEES AS PEERS**

Stg. 10

**HIRE THE SELF-MOTIVATED**
Self motivated people are more flexible as they not only take initiative and stay motivated without supervision but also handle ambiguity better. If they are treated like peers they will take responsibility for their actions

Stg. 11

**ELIMINATE FANCY PERKS**
Perks create division and send signals that some people are better than others. Get rid of perks such as reserved car parking space, special washrooms and/or dinning rooms, etc.

Stg. 12

**ENCOURAGE INFORMALLITY**
Call everyone by their first names as it will eliminate any chance of drawing attention to status by calling Mr. or Ms. which in turn can create barriers to communication.

**Fig. 2.19: Strategies for Viewing Employees as Peers**

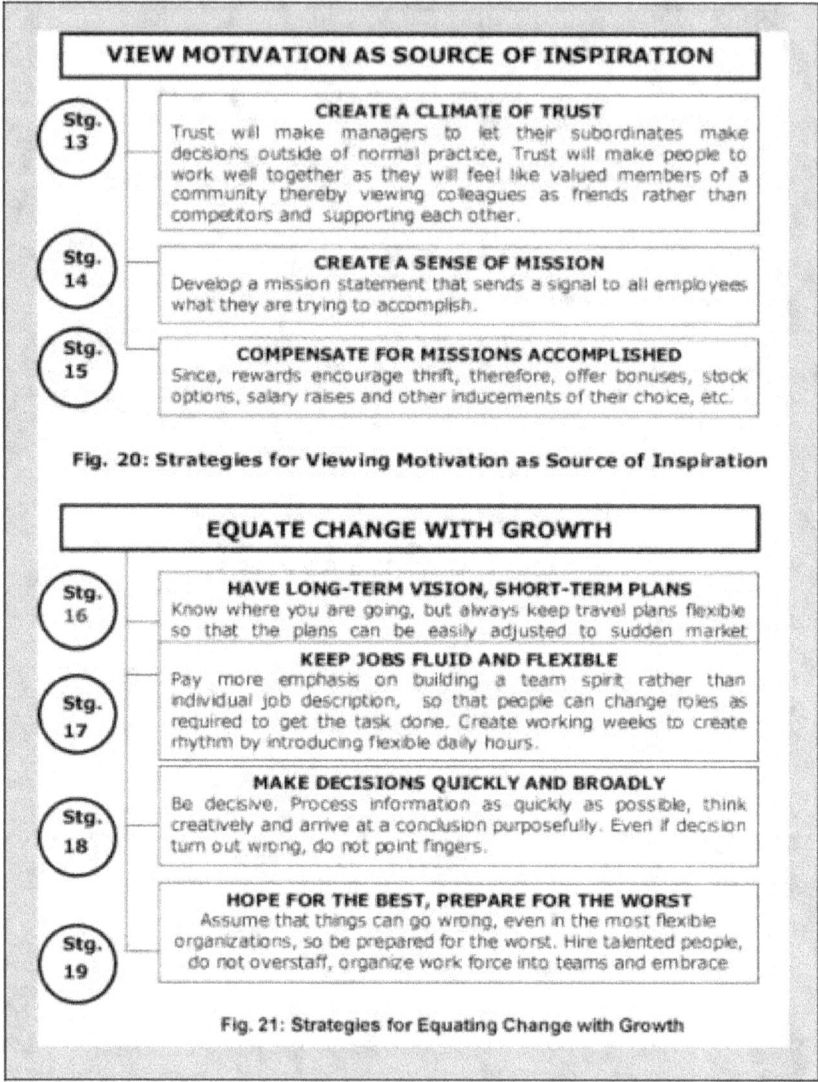

### VIEW MOTIVATION AS SOURCE OF INSPIRATION

**Stg. 13**

**CREATE A CLIMATE OF TRUST**
Trust will make managers to let their subordinates make decisions outside of normal practice, Trust will make people to work well together as they will feel like valued members of a community thereby viewing colleagues as friends rather than competitors and supporting each other.

**Stg. 14**

**CREATE A SENSE OF MISSION**
Develop a mission statement that sends a signal to all employees what they are trying to accomplish.

**Stg. 15**

**COMPENSATE FOR MISSIONS ACCOMPLISHED**
Since, rewards encourage thrift, therefore, offer bonuses, stock options, salary raises and other inducements of their choice, etc.

Fig. 20: Strategies for Viewing Motivation as Source of Inspiration

### EQUATE CHANGE WITH GROWTH

**Stg. 16**

**HAVE LONG-TERM VISION, SHORT-TERM PLANS**
Know where you are going, but always keep travel plans flexible so that the plans can be easily adjusted to sudden market

**Stg. 17**

**KEEP JOBS FLUID AND FLEXIBLE**
Pay more emphasis on building a team spirit rather than individual job description, so that people can change roles as required to get the task done. Create working weeks to create rhythm by introducing flexible daily hours.

**Stg. 18**

**MAKE DECISIONS QUICKLY AND BROADLY**
Be decisive. Process information as quickly as possible, think creatively and arrive at a conclusion purposefully. Even if decision turn out wrong, do not point fingers.

**Stg. 19**

**HOPE FOR THE BEST, PREPARE FOR THE WORST**
Assume that things can go wrong, even in the most flexible organizations, so be prepared for the worst. Hire talented people, do not overstaff, organize work force into teams and embrace

Fig. 21: Strategies for Equating Change with Growth

**Fig. 22: Strategies for Re-Building Corporate Culture**

Fig. 2.23 shows a model of the strategy to use the E-mail whereas Fig. 2.24 shows the strategy to improve the balance of an effective worker.

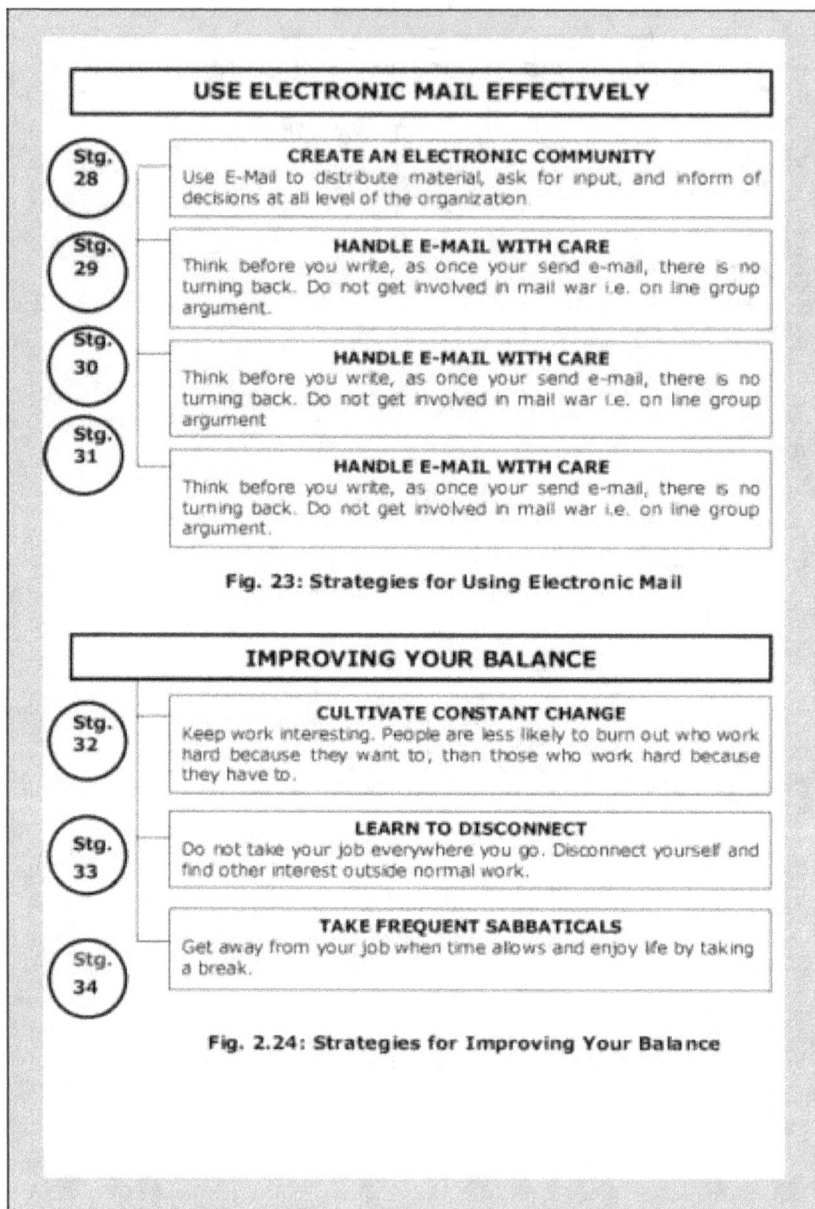

**USE ELECTRONIC MAIL EFFECTIVELY**

Stg. 28

**CREATE AN ELECTRONIC COMMUNITY**
Use E-Mail to distribute material, ask for input, and inform of decisions at all level of the organization.

Stg. 29

**HANDLE E-MAIL WITH CARE**
Think before you write, as once your send e-mail, there is no turning back. Do not get involved in mail war i.e. on line group argument.

Stg. 30

**HANDLE E-MAIL WITH CARE**
Think before you write, as once your send e-mail, there is no turning back. Do not get involved in mail war i.e. on line group argument

Stg. 31

**HANDLE E-MAIL WITH CARE**
Think before you write, as once your send e-mail, there is no turning back. Do not get involved in mail war i.e. on line group argument.

**Fig. 23: Strategies for Using Electronic Mail**

**IMPROVING YOUR BALANCE**

Stg. 32

**CULTIVATE CONSTANT CHANGE**
Keep work interesting. People are less likely to burn out who work hard because they want to, than those who work hard because they have to.

Stg. 33

**LEARN TO DISCONNECT**
Do not take your job everywhere you go. Disconnect yourself and find other interest outside normal work.

Stg. 34

**TAKE FREQUENT SABBATICALS**
Get away from your job when time allows and enjoy life by taking a break.

**Fig. 2.24: Strategies for Improving Your Balance**

## 6.20   BUILDING A HIGH–TRUST ORGANIZATION

In today's global competitive market, corporations need to be flexible so that they can effectively adapt to constant change. However, to implement modern trends and initiative demanding changes (such as empowerment, reengineering, downsizing, flattened organization, organizational learning, and cross-functional teamwork, etc.) a solid foundation of trust is vital for any progressive organization. Robert Bruce Shaw in his book "Trust in the Balance" published by Jossey-Bass Inc., San Fransisco, has beautifully described and explained (a) the three imperatives of trust, (b) leverage points for building trust and (c) Low-trust situations.

The author has adapted these in the following models. The three imperatives of trust are shown in Fig. 2.25, leverage points for building trusts are shown in Fig. 2.26, and low-trust situations are shown in Fig. 2.27.

## 6.21  CONCLDING REMARKS

To achieve strategic goals and objectives, strategy implementation is the translation of chosen strategy into organizational action. Strategy implementation is the manner in which an organization should develop, utilize, and amalgamate organizational culture, organizational structure, organizational control systems, and to follow strategies that lead to competitive advantage and a better performance of the organization.

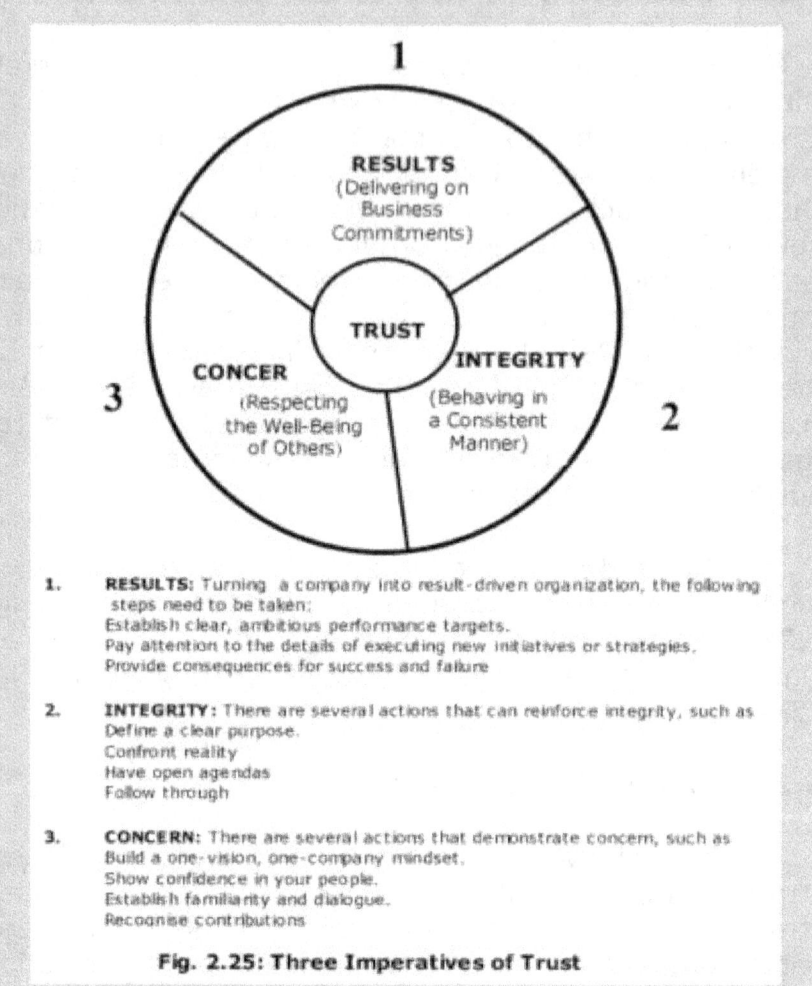

1. **RESULTS:** Turning a company into result-driven organization, the following steps need to be taken:
   Establish clear, ambitious performance targets.
   Pay attention to the details of executing new initiatives or strategies.
   Provide consequences for success and failure

2. **INTEGRITY:** There are several actions that can reinforce integrity, such as
   Define a clear purpose.
   Confront reality
   Have open agendas
   Follow through

3. **CONCERN:** There are several actions that demonstrate concern, such as
   Build a one-vision, one-company mindset.
   Show confidence in your people.
   Establish familiarity and dialogue.
   Recognise contributions

### Fig. 2.25: Three Imperatives of Trust

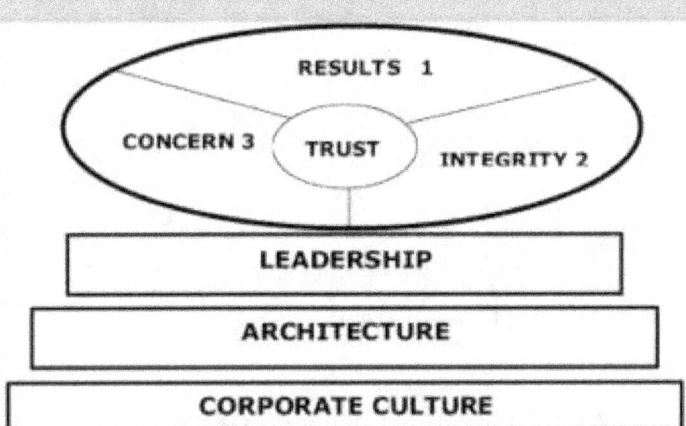

1. **LEADERSHIP:** Trust begins and ends with the actions of leaders. Leader must do the following:
   - Model the three imperative himself (or herself).
   - Build trustworthy leadership teams.
   - Develop trust-sustaining organization mechanisms (including corporate principles, structures, and procedures.

2. **ARCHITECTURE:** Architecture should support autonomy. To ensure that your Organizational architecture reinforces rather than undermines trust, take the following actions:
   - Develop aggressive business targets.
   - Develop aligned performance accountabilities
   - Ensure superior talent at every level.
   - Maintain systems to share information
   - Institute a few rigorous strategic controls

3. **CORPORATE CULTURE:** Organizational life involving the power of vision, values, symbols, operating principles and norms, etc. is equally important to sustain trust. to develop the appropriate culture, take following actions:
   - Develop a common vision and shared view about competitive realities.
   - Live by genuinely felt values and operating principles..
   - Build familiarity across all levels of the organizational units.
   - Encourage an environment of risk taking and experimentation.

**Fig. 2.26: Leverage Points for Building Trust**

# Role of Strategic Management in Business Organizations

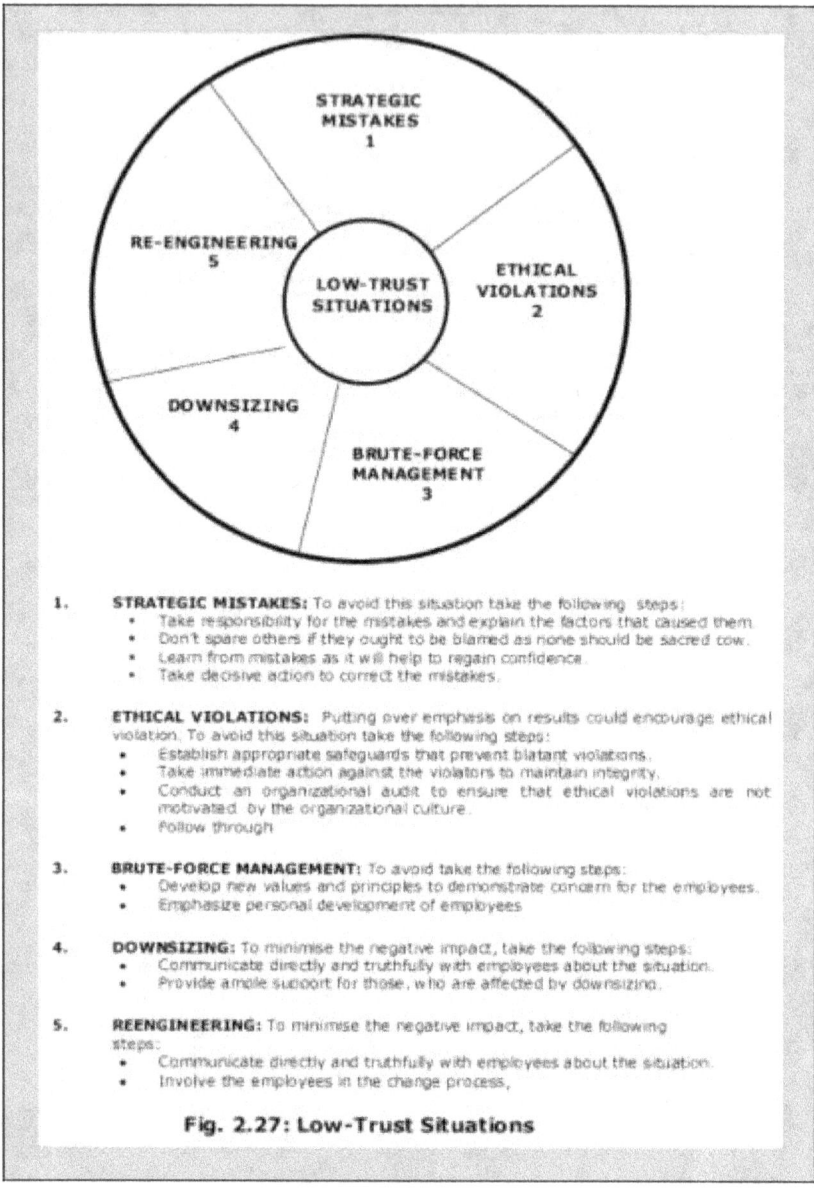

1. **STRATEGIC MISTAKES:** To avoid this situation take the following steps:
   - Take responsibility for the mistakes and explain the factors that caused them.
   - Don't spare others if they ought to be blamed as none should be sacred cow.
   - Learn from mistakes as it will help to regain confidence.
   - Take decisive action to correct the mistakes.

2. **ETHICAL VIOLATIONS:** Putting over emphasis on results could encourage ethical violation. To avoid this situation take the following steps:
   - Establish appropriate safeguards that prevent blatant violations.
   - Take immediate action against the violators to maintain integrity.
   - Conduct an organizational audit to ensure that ethical violations are not motivated by the organizational culture.
   - Follow through

3. **BRUTE-FORCE MANAGEMENT:** To avoid take the following steps:
   - Develop new values and principles to demonstrate concern for the employees.
   - Emphasize personal development of employees

4. **DOWNSIZING:** To minimise the negative impact, take the following steps:
   - Communicate directly and truthfully with employees about the situation.
   - Provide ample support for those, who are affected by downsizing.

5. **REENGINEERING:** To minimise the negative impact, take the following steps:
   - Communicate directly and truthfully with employees about the situation.
   - Involve the employees in the change process.

**Fig. 2.27: Low-Trust Situations**

Organizational culture refers to the specialized collection of values, attitudes, norms and beliefs shared by organizational members and groups, whilst organizational structure allocates special value developing tasks and roles to the employees and states how these tasks and roles can be correlated so as maximize efficiency, quality, and customer satisfaction-the pillars of competitive advantage. However, organizational structure is not sufficient in itself to motivate the employees, therefore an organizational control system is also required as this control system equips managers with motivational incentives for employees as well as feedback on employees and organizational performance.

Implementing a strategy may be considered as six stepped process, such as: (i) developing an organization having potential of carrying out strategy successfully; (ii) disbursement of abundant resources to strategy-essential activities; (iii) creating strategy-encouraging policies; (iv) employing best policies and programmes for improvement; (v) linking reward structure to accomplishment of results; and (vi) making use of strategic leadership.

It must be kept in mind that even excellently formulated strategies are liable to failure, if they are not properly implemented, thereby making it essential to understand that strategy implementation is not possible unless there is stability between strategy and each organizational dimension such as: organizational structure; reward structure; and resource-allocation process, etc. Also, strategy implementation may pose a threat to many managers and employees in an organization leading to conflicts in the organization. For example, new power relationships are predicted and achieved and new groups (formal as well as informal) are formed whose values, attitudes, beliefs and concerns may not be known; and with the change in power and status roles, the managers and employees may employ confrontation behaviour.

# Chapter 7

## STRATEGIC MANAGEMENT FROM ISLAMIC PERSPECTIVES

### 7.1    INTRODUCTION

There is an Islamic perspective to management. In Islam, believers are to conform to the teachings of the Quran and the Sunnah of Prophet Muhammad (SAW)[35]. Among Allah's creation, Man is the best and elevated to the rank of Allah's khalifah (vicegerent) on the Earth. As a khalifah, the Man has responsibilty to prosper the earth one lives on, thereby never stops striving to improve oneself and one's community.

The Quran exhorts believers to continuously enjoin good and forbid evil, wheras Prophet Mhammad (SAW) has been depicted as possessing the attribute of altruism, meaning "sincerest concern for the well-being of others", embracing the attitude and practice of caring, sharing, nurturing and bonding in one's relationship with others. It connotes: unselfish orientation towards the welfare of people; mindful of the feelings and needs of those around us; and always striving for win-win situations in life.

In its socio-economic context, it is the antithesis of absolute capitalism, one-upmanship, survival of the fittest, and manipulation of others. The world today is so corruptible, gullible and materialistic that many

---

[35] Salle Allah Wasalam (SAW)

nations and corporations operate without a soul or conscience mindedness. By and large, the capitalistic bottom-line of maximising profits has become the benchmark for purported success, pervading local, regional, national, and international organisational levels.

## 7.2   NEED FOR MANAGEMENT PARADIGM

there is a dire need for management paradigm that transcends narrow chauvinism, neo-conservatism and jingoism – with a universal, egalitarian and magnanimous approach.This managerial approach is still regarded as a pragmatic model that can be used to get things done efficaciously.

For example, Theodore Levitt of Harvard described management as "the rational assessment of a situation and the systematic selection of goals and purposes (what is to be done?); the systematic development of strategies to achieve these goals; the marshalling of the required resources; the rational design, organisation, direction, and control of the activities required to attain the selected purposes; and finally, the motivating and rewarding of people to do the work."

Michael Hart's *The 100: A ranking of the Most Influential Persons in History* (1978), mentions the uniqueness of Prophet Muhammad's leadership, placing the Prophet (SAW) as the most influential leader in human history, whilst presenting the qualities of a leader who was a successful businessman, a spiritual reformer, a charismatic commander, a just administrator, a peace negotiator, a political strategist, a jurist, a wise counsellor, and a prescient statesman in his lifetime.

## 7.3 MANAGEMENT FROM ISLAMIC PERSPECTIVE

As in the days of Prophet Muhammad (SAW), modern management needs strong leadership and excellent organiZational capabilities to achieve exponential success. The super-ordinate paradigm of leadership provided by Prophet Muhammad (SAW) can be explained by a three-dimensional orientation, fusing alignment, attunement and empowerment in organisational development. When these three dimensions are cast, the outcome will be organisational synergy, the framework within which the strategic altruistic mindset should operate and the future can be positively mapped. Such an alignment constitutes an organisation's vision of greatness. It is the direction-setting aspect of leadership, the inductive process (as opposed to the conventional deductive process) that formulates vision and mission statements. It describes the business, the technology it envelopes, the methodology it pursues, and the culture it embraces.

Alignment implies that everyone in the organisation is moving towards the same objective, each in agreement with the other. Where adjustments have to be made, the parties involved will sit in mutual consultation to resolve issues. In Prophet Muhammad's leadership paradigm, alignment is synonymous with Tawheed (the Oneness of God), which is tempered by Iman (belief) and Taqwa (God-fearing). If people within an organisation is God-conscious, have strong faith and adhere to a firm set of values, then the stage is set for greatness in every field. Attunement is the esprit de corps, the will, the emotions, the passion and the compassion that fires the process towards goal attainment, when attunement has to move in tandem with alignment.

In Prophet Muhammad's leadership model, attunement means ibadah – righteous deeds performed daily as acts of faith. When employees of an organisation continuously perform good deeds and shun bad behaviour, the environment becomes harmonious, thereby achieving best results. There is a tendency to be committed, truthful and loyal because they continuously perform acts of quality in daily work. Empowerment is the willingness to allow skilled and knowledgeable people to use their talents and energies at work. Quite often, organisations and even nations falter in the face of stiff competition or when adjusting to new technology because leaders are not confident in the abilities of their people. Such people feel de-motivated. But when alignment, attunement and empowerment are employed in strategic human resource development, people perform because they feel wanted and appreciated.

When management accords employees the right to share the organizational vision and mission, a purposeful sense of direction is communicated to all levels. Responsibility and authority get delegated; and as long as people's responses are consistent with the vision and mission statements, conflict will not arise because everyone would be gunning for the same target. Empowerment ensures down-liners are allowed the initiative and freedom to realise their full potential by planning, organising and controlling their activities for the good of their organisation, whilst synergy is derived from the old Greek word synergein, which means working together with heart and soul. Synergism is the result of simultaneous actions of separate agencies, creating a greater total effect than the sum of their individual efforts. Synergy is the extraordinary outcome of aligned, attuned and empowered people with shared values in action. It is the energy that flows through a team of people, producing greater performance.

In Prophet Muhammad's governance model, synergy implies movement towards al-falah (the forces of success and prosperity). Attunement, coupled with empowerment, involves consultation, motivation and building esprit de corps among team members, thereby involving the emotions, the intellect and commitment from the heart (istiqamah). When Prophet Muhammad (SAW) involved his players actively in the process of problem-solving and decision-making, everyone was enlightened about the opportunities, hardships, and dangers involved in the many campaigns against the enemy. Morale-wise, when decisions were made by mutual consultation or consensus, they not only increased the speed and efficiency of actual operations but also fostered a high degree of trust and support in the followers, providing them with a raison d'etre for their ongoing military expeditions. Every member becomes totally committed to the cause.

## 7.4 IDEAS REGARDING ISLAMIC PERSPECTIVES TO STRATEGIC MANAGEMENT

The primary revealed knowledge source is the Holy Quran. This basic source is elaborated through the Ahadith - the traditions and the Sunnah, the actions of the Prophet (SAW). Also Islamic scholars treat Fiqh, the science of Islamic jurisprudence, as a source of revealed knowledge too.

Other sources are the reported sayings and actions of the first four Khulfa, often referred to Khulafa–Er-Rashdine (RAA)[36]; instances from Islamic history; studies in Islamic administration and management; studies in Islamic social sciences; studies in Islamic culture; writings of leading Islamic scholars;

---

[36] Rahmat Allah Alle

and the writings of leading and authentic non-Muslim scholars.

## 7.4.1 Management: Islamic Perspectives

Islam means "The Surrender", that is, men surrendering to God have will and purpose. Islam is an Arabic word that connotes submission, surrender and obedience. As a religion, Islam stands for complete submission and obedience to Allah [SWT][37]. Another literal meaning of the word Islam is 'peace' and this connotes that one can achieve real peace of body and mind only through submission and obedience to Allah [SWT]. Islam consists of submission and obedience to Allah [SWT], the Lord of the universe.

Managing an organization is a skilful job and today, globally operated organizations are faced with numerous challenges. How corporate leaders should approach their obligations is one of the important queries at the desk of business researchers. Surrendering to Allah's instructions inculcates humility, responsibility and self-accountability among organizational leaders to fulfill their duties at their best. Holistic approach to organizational management provides corporate leaders with more options to deal with issues innovatively. Islamic management model is flexible enough to adapt according to the circumstances for maximum outcome of the organization.

## 7.4.2 Islamic Management Vs. Conventional Management

The Islamic approach to management is an emerging discipline, often referred to as Islamic management, looks at the management of organizations from the perspective of the knowledge

---

[37] Subhana Wa Talla [SWT]

from the revealed sources and other Islamic sources of knowledge and results in applications compatible with the Islamic beliefs and practices.

The comparison of Islamic management with the conventional management on varios base is shown in Fig. 2.28.

| BASES | ISLAMIC MANAGEMENT | CONVENTIONAL MANAGEMENT |
|---|---|---|
| Paradigm guiding management of organizations | No demarcation between the secular and the religious; human life is an organic whole; all human activity can be Ibadah provided they are guided by Allah's commandments | Clear demarcation between the secular and the religious; human activities are separated; spiritual or religious aspect is a private matter of individuals while work is in public domain |
| PURPOSE OF HUMAN: existence dictating management of organizations | Purpose of human existence is to obey and fulfill Allah's commandments and act as the vice-regent of Allah on earth. | Purpose of human existence is to utilize natural resources to satisfy one's needs, wants and desires and to remain happy |
| Purpose of organization | Organizations are meant to be groups of people coming together for attaining the purpose of human existence. | Organizations are meant to be groups of people coming together to attain the organizational goals |
| Nature of organizational objectives | Organizational objectives are both economic and non-economic and are subservient to larger purpose of human existence | Organizational objectives are both economic and non-economic in nature and are subservient to organizational interests |
| SOURCE OF ETHICS AND VALUES: governing management of organizations | The revealed knowledge and the traditions of the Prophet (SAW) constitute the ultimate source of business ethics and personal values | Ethics is relative and values are derived from multiple sources such as upbringing, society, and experiences. Ethics could be relative as in utilitarian theory |
| Organizational Control | Organizational control has to operate in a way designed to make the human being subservient to the will of Allah [SWT] | Organizational control has to operate in a way designed to align human objectives with the organizational objectives |
| Locus of control | The locus of control is internal. Each person is responsible and accountable for his actions | The locus of control is external and lies in the realm of the organization |
| Organizational responsibility and accountability | Human being has choice, free will and freedom of action therefore is responsible and accountable for all actions | Responsibility and accountability vested in the chief executive who dele-gates it. Employees controlled through organizational systems to ensure responsibility and accountability |

**Fig. 2.28**

### 7.4.3 Operations Management from Islamic Perspective

Management characterizes the process of leading and directing all or part of an organization, often a business, through the deployment and manipulation of resources (human, financial, material, intellectual or intangible).

From western perspective, they usually emphasize on seeking tremendous profits regardless how they get it. They will do what ever it takes in order to achieve their targets. The main thing for them is profit maximization. Whereas, the Islamic approach to management it is an emerging discipline, often referred to as Islamic management, looks at the management of organizations from the perspective of the knowledge from the revealed sources and other Islamic sources of knowledge and results in applications compatible with the Islamic beliefs and practices.

The focus of Islamic management of quality and excellence is man (human resource) and not profit maximization. In other words, Islam put emphasize on balancing worldly and hereafter matters not just only aiming for the profits. They often do it in a right way. No negative elements insert to it. All things are done inline with Islamic guideline. Resources means that a natural, human, or manufactured item that helps a produce goods and services; a productive agent or factor of production.

In Islamic perspectives, all resources are provided by Allah [SWT] and us as a Khalifah is not the owner of all the resources. According to Quran 2:29, "the resources are for the benefit of all and not just a few". Thus, it means that all human being must utilize the resources equally. Besides that, everyone also must acquired the resources rightfully, in manner that already indicated by the Quran and Sunnah and not cause any damage and inconvenience to the people and society in general.

# Chapter 8

## 25 CASE STUDIES ON STRATEGIC MANAGEMENT

### CASE STUDY 1:

BB Ltd., is a business organized as three divisions and head office. The divisions are based on market groupings, which are retail, wholesale and Government. The divisions do not trade with each other. The main method of control of the divisions has been the requirement to earn a return on investment (ROI) of 15% p.a. The definition of return and capital employed is provided by head office, at the criterion ROI rate of 15%. The recent experience of BB Ltd, is that the group as a whole has been able to earn the 15% but there have been wide variations between the results obtained by different division.

This infringes another group policy that forbids cross-subsidization, i.e. each and every division must earn the criterion ROI. BB Ltd is now considering divestment strategies and this could include the closure of one or more of its divisions. The head office is aware that the Boston Product Market Portfolio Matrix (BPMPM) is widely used within the divisions in the formulation and review of marketing strategies.

As it is so widely known within the group and is generally regarded by the divisions as being useful, the head office is considering employing this approach to assist in the divestment decision.

## Evaluation of the use of the concept of ROI by BB Ltd.

**Question:** How you would evaluate the use by BB Ltd. of the concept of ROI and its policy that forbids cross-subsidization?

**Answer:** ROI is an accounting measure that estimates the level of profits as a proportion of the capital employed over the year. The concept of ROI is widely used by different companies to measures its performance. Therefore BB Ltd. Is not unusual in using this concept of ROI as a means of performance monitoring of its different divisions. Perhaps on division of BB Ltd., may have failed to meet its ROI because it might have recently purchased new fixed assets. Perhaps another division might be using old assets that have been written off. Further one division might be riskier than another division. Regarding ROI and cross subsidization: There could be a lot of problems with cross subsidy.

This issue of cross subsidies is more complex than it first appears. We do not know how the investment funds have been allocated if the head office allocates them, and the divisions cannot take their own investment decisions, there is a cross subsidization by the back door as it were. Further one division's hard earned cash might be used to buy another division's assets. Arguably, cross-subsidization is the advantage of a business like BB Ltd. Further, if the businesses have different business cycle, they are able to bail each other out when appropriate, whilst ensuring that the shareholders receive a fairly constant return.

## Application of BPMPM by BB Ltd In its divestment decision:

**Question:** Describe the extent to which the BPMPM could be applied by BB Ltd in its divestment decision and evaluate the appropriateness of the use of the BPMPM for this purpose?

**Answer:** BPMPM aims to link the overall growth of the market for a product, the growth in the market share of a product, with the product's cash-generative activities. BPMPM classifies a company's products in terms of potential cash generation and cash expenditure requirements into cash cows, dogs, stars and question marks: (a) cash cows need very little capital expenditure and generate high level of cash income. The important strategic feature of cash cows is that they are already generating high cash returns that can be used to finance the stars. (b) stars are products with a high share of a high growth market. In short term, term require capital expenditure, in excess of the cash they generate, in order to maintain their market position, but promise high returns in the future and in due course, however, stars will become cash cows, which are characterized by a high market share, but low sales growth; (c) dogs products with a low share of a low growth market. Dogs should be allowed to die, or should be killed off; and (d) question marks are products in a high-growth market, but where they have a low market share and a decision needs to be taken about whether the products justify considerable capital expenditure in the hope of increasing their market share, or whether they should be allowed dying quietly.

Regarging appropriateness of use of BPMPM, BPMP is conventionally assumed to apply to products and it is perhaps unusual to see it applied to businesses and divisions. The problem is that we do not know enough about the firm's product range to suggest how the matrix could be applied. Rather than assuming that a whole division is a dog and divesting it, is possible that a through review of the product range of each division could be examined to see whether certain products can be pruned from the range. BPMPM should not be used in isolation and it needs to be modified from time to time.

## Models for making a divestment decision

**Question:** Recommend, and justify, two other models that could be used in making a divestment decision and demonstrate how BB Ltd could utilize these models to make this decision.?

**Answer:** A no. of models is available, which could be used by the company in making a divestment decision. Two such models could be used: (a) porter's five forces model and the product life cycle. Porter's five forces model can be used to place each division in the competitive context and in this context, the five forces model suggests that the competitive environment is determined by five factors, namely: (i) the threat of new entrants; (ii) the threat of substitute products; (ii) the bargaining power of customers; (iv) the bargaining power of suppliers; and (v) the state of competitive rivalry within the industry.

The value of this model is that it examines each division's strengths in a competitive context and if the trend is for entry barriers to get lower, or if a major new entrant is no the horizon, this must influence the divestment decision, if the business is a marginal player in the market or if the resources required to fight off such a challenge are too expensive. Likewise, if the customers are powerful or suppliers are powerful, then the margins would get eroded steadily and firm's business would become less attractive. Similarly if the threat of substitute products becomes serious, then divestment might become a sensible choice.

With respect to the Product Life Cycle model bears similarities to the BCG matrix. This model suggests that a firm's products have a natural life cycle that can be analyzed into the phases of introduction, growth, maturity and decline. In the introduction phase, the product still has to make money. In the growth phase, it starts to make profit. Maturity occurs when the demand is no longer growing. The demand and the profit are at its peak. In the decline phase, demand falls off, profits fall and eventually no profits are made. Thus BB Ltd can use this model to examine the condition of the products in each of the divisions.

## CASE STUDY 2:

DD is the India's premier public service broadcaster with more than 1,000 transmitters covering 90% of the country's population across on estimated 70 million homes. It has more than 20,000 employees managing its metro and regional channels. Recent years have seen growing competition from many private channels numbering more than 65, and the cable and satellite operators (C & S). The C & S network reaches nearly 30 million homes and is growing at a very fast rate. DD's business model is based on selling half – hour slots of commercial time to the programme producers and charging them a minimum guarantee.

For instance, the present tariff for the first 20 episodes of a programme Rps.30 lakhs plus the cost of production of the programme. In exchange the procedures get 780 seconds of commercial time that he can sell to advertisers and can generate revenue. Break-even point for procedures, at the present rates, thus is Rs.75,000 for a 10 second advertising spot. Beyond 20 episodes, the minimum guarantee is Rps.65 lakhs for which the procedures has to charge Rps.1,15,000 for a 10 second spot in order to break-even. It is at this point the advertisers face a problem – the competitive rates for a 10 second spot is Rps.50,000. Procedures are possessive about buying commercial time on DD.

As a result the DD's projected growth of revenue is only commercial time on DD. As a result the DD's projected growth of revenue is only 6-10% as against 50-60% for the private sector channels. Software suppliers, advertisers and audiences are deserting DD owing to its unrealistic pricing policy. DD has options before it. First, it should privates, second it should remain purely public service broadcaster and third, a middle path. The challenge seems to be exploit DD's immense potential and emerge as a formidable player in the mass media.

### Best Option for DD

**Question:** What is the best option, in your view, for DD?

**Answer:** For several years Doordarshan was the only broadcaster of television programmes in India. After the opening of the sector to the private entrepreneur (cable and satellite channels), the market has witnessed major changes. The number of channels have increased and also the quality of programmes, backed by technology, has improved. In terms of quality of programmers, opportunity to advertise, outreach activities, the broadcasting has become a popular business. Broadcasters too have realised the great business potential in the market. But for this, policies need to be rationalised and be opened to the scope of innovativeness not only in term of quality of programmes. This would not come by simply going to more areas or by allowing bureaucratic set up to continue in the organisation.

Strategically the DD needs to undergo a policy overhaul. DD, out of three options, namely privatisation, public service broadcaster or a middle path, can choose the third one, i.e. a combination of both. The whole privatisation is not possible under the diversified political scenario. Nor it would be desirable to hand over the broadcasting emotively in the private hand as it proves to be a great means of communication of many socially oriented public programmers. The government could also think in term of creating a corporation (as it did by creating Prasar Bharti) and provide reasonable autonomy to DD. So far as its advertisement tariff is concerned that can be made fairly competitive. However, at the same time cost of advertising is to be compared with the reach enjoyed by the doordarshan. The number of viewers may be far more to justify higher tariffs.

### SWOT Factors Analysis

**Question:** Analyse the SWOT factors the DD has?

**Answer:** The SWOT analyses involves study of strengths, weaknesses, opportunities and threats of an organisation. SWOT factors that are evidently available to the Doordarshan are: S – Strength: (a) more than 1000 transmitters; (b) covering 90% of population across 70 million homes against only 30 million home by C & S; (c) More than 20,000 employees. W – Weakness: (a) rigid pricing strategy; (b) low credibility with certain sections of society; and (c) quality of program's is not as good as compared to C & S network. O– Opportunities: (a) infrastructure can be leased out to cable and satellite channel; (b) digital terrestrial transmission; (c) regional focused channels; (d) allotment of time, slots to other broadcasters. T – Threats: (a) desertion of advertisers and producers may result in loss of revenues; due to quality of program the reach of C & S network is continuously expanding as the C & S network need the trained staff, some employees of DD may switchover and take new jobs; (d) best of the market-technology is being used by the private channels.

## In Suppoer of Proposed Alternative

**Question:** Why do you think that the proposed alternative is the best?

**Answer:** It is suggested that the DD should adopt a middle path. It should have a mix of both the options. It should economized on its operational aspects and ensure more productivity in term of revenue generation and optimisation of use of its infrastructure. Wherever, the capacities are underutilised, these may be leased out to the private operations. At the same time quality and viewership of programmes should be improved. Bureaucracy may reduce new strategic initiatives or make the organisation less transparent. Complete privatisation can fetch a good sum and may solve many of the managerial and operational problems. However, complete public monopoly is not advisable because that denies the government to fully exploit the avenue for social and public use. The government will also lose out as it will not be able to take advantage of rising potential of the market.

## CASE STUDY 3:

Dr. Sukumar inherited his father's Dey's Lab in Delhi in 1995. Till 2002, he owned 4 labs in the National Capital Region (NCR). His ambition was to turn it into a National chain. The number increased to 7 in 2003 across the country, including the acquisition of Platinum lab in Mumbai. The number is likely to go to 50 within 2-3 years from 21 at present. Infusion of Rps. 28 crores for a 26% stake by Pharma Capital has its growth strategy. The lab with a revenue of Rps. 75 crores is among top three Pathological labs in India with Atlantic (Rps. 77 crores) and Pacific (Rps. 55 crores). Yet its market share is only 2% of Rs. 3,500 crores market. The top 3 firms command only 6% as against 40-45% by their counterparts in the USA. There are about 20,000 to 1,00,000 stand alone labs engaged in routine pathological business in India, with no system of mandatory licensing and registration. That is why Dr. Sukumar has not gone for acquisition or joint ventures. He does not find many existing laboratories meeting quality standards. His six labs have been accredited nationally whereon many large hospitals have not thought of accreditation.

The College of American pathologists accreditation of Dey's lab would help it to reach clients outside India. In Dey's Lab, the bio-chemistry and blood testing equipments are sanitised every day. The bar coding and automated registration of patients do not allow any identity mix-ups. Even routine tests are conducted with highly sophisticated systems. Technical expertise enables them to carry out 1650 variety of tests. Same day reports are available for samples reaching by 3 p.m. and by 7 a.m. next day for samples from 500 collection centres located across the country. Their technicians work round the clock, unlike competitors. Home services for collection and reporting is also available. There is a huge unutilised capacity.

Now it is trying to top other segments. 20% of its total business comes through its main laboratory which acts as a reference lab for many leading hospitals. New mega labs are being built to Encash preclinical and multi-centre clinical trials within India and provide postgraduate training to the pathologists.

### Vision and Mission

**Question:** What do you understand by the term Vision? What is the difference between 'Vision' and Mission'? What vision Dr. Sukumar had at the time of inheritance of Dey's Lab? Has it been achieved?

**Answer:** A Strategic vision is a road map of a company's future – providing specifics about technology and customer focus, the geographic and product markets to be pursued, the capabilities it plans to develop, and the kind of company that management is trying to create. A strategic vision thus points an organisation in a particular direction, charts a strategic path for it to follow in preparing for the future, and moulds organizational identity. A company's Mission statement is typically focused on its present business scope – "who we are and what we do". Mission statements broadly describe an organisation's present capabilities, customer focus, activities, and business makeup. Mission is also an expression of the vision of the corporation.

To make the vision come alive and become relevant, it needs to be spelt out. It is through the mission that the firm spells out its vision. Dr. Sukumar's vision at the initial stage was to turn his one pathological laboratory firm into a national chain of pathological laboratories. He is in the process of achieving the vision as a number of Labs have been opened and others are in pipeline. However, at the same time the market share is low when compared with the external benchmark from US market.

## Adequacy of Business Strategy for Growth

**Question:** For growth what business strategy has been adopted by Dr. Sukumar?

**Answer:** To a large extent Dr. Dey's Lab has opted the business strategy of internal growth rather than going in for acquisitions or joint ventures. The reason for such a strategy is that Dr. Sukumar does not find many existing laboratories meeting the quality standards. To fund its growth and raise funds it has also given a 26% stake to Pharma Capital.

## Marketing Strategy Of Dr. Sukumar

**Question:** What is the marketing strategy of Dr. Sukumar to overtake its competitors?

**Answer:** Dr. Sukumar's marketing strategy is superior to its competitors. Over a period of time it is able to evolve itself as reference lab for many leading hospitals. This is a testimony of the level of confidence it enjoys among the medical professionals. It provides a high level of customer services because of: (a) Product mix: It possesses technical expertise to conduct 1650 variety of tests; (b) Quality: The laboratories use modern methods to conduct tests. Even routine tests are conducted with highly sophisticated procedures. Technology such as bar coding and automated registration of patients is also used. Thus there are no mistakes in the identity of samples. There is also daily sanitisation and validation of lab equipments; (c) Speed: Laboratories are working round-the-clock. Further, using modern systems the company is able to deliver test results faster; and Convenience: There are 500 collection centres for the laboratory, thereby the reach is more. Additionally, system of collection of samples from home also provide convenience to the patients and others.

### Weakness in Dr. Sukumar's Business Strategy

**Question:** In your opinion what could be the biggest weakness in Dr. Sukumar's business strategy?

**Answer:** A weakness is an inherent limitation or constraint of the organisation which creates strategic disadvantage to it. In the case it is given that Dr Sukumar has not gone for mergers and acquisition as he does not find many prospective laboratories meeting the quality standards. Thus its biggest weakness is its inability to capitalise the opportunities through mergers and acquisitions. Acquisitions and partnerships can help in leveraging the existing goodwill. Many of these labs must be enjoying a lot of goodwill in their region. In fact, a business in the medical field such as a pathological laboratory, trust and faith are important. On account of its size and available resources Dey's Lab could have easily acquired some of these labs and built upon their names. With resources it should be feasible to modernize them to make them compatible with the business ideology and quality systems of the Dey's Lab. However, it appears that the company lacked capability to modernise an existing laboratory.

### CASE STUDY 4:

In 2006-07 PTC Food division decided to enter the fast growing (20-30% annually) snacks segment, an altogether new to it. It had only one national competitor-Trepsico's Trito. After a year its wafer snack brand-Ringo, fetched 20% market share across the country. Ringo's introduction was coincided with the cricket world cup. The wafer snacks market is estimated to be around Rps. 250 crores. The company could take the advantage of its existing distribution network and also source potatoes from farmers easily. Before the PTC could enter the market a cross-functional team made a customer survey through a marketing research group in 14 cities of the country to know about the snacks of eating habits of people. The result showed that the customers within the age-group of 15-24 years were the most promising for the product as they were quite enthusiastic about experimenting new snack taste. The company reported to its chefs and the chefs came out with 16 flavours with varying tastes suiting to the targetted age-group.

The company decided to target the youngsters as primary target on the assumption that once they are lured in, it was easier to reach the whole family. Advertising in this category was extremely crowded. Every week two-three local products in new names were launched, sometimes with similar names. To break through this clutter the company decided to bank upon humour appeal. The Industry sources reveal that PTC spent about Rps. 50 crores on advertisement and used all possible mediaprint and electronic, both including the creation of its own website, Ringoringoyoungo.com with offers of online games, contests etc. Mobile phone tone downloading was also planned which proved very effective among teenagers.

The site was advertised on all dotcom networks. Em TV, Shine TV, Bee TV and other important channels were also used for its advertisement along with FM radio channels in about 60 cities with large hoardings at strategic places. Analysts believes that Ringo's success story owes a lot to PTC's widespread distribution channels and aggressive advertisements. Humour appeal was a big success.

The `Ringo' was made visible by painting the Railway bogies passing across the States. It has also been successful to induce Lovely Brothers' Future Group to replace Trito in their Big-Bazaar and chain of food Bazaars. PTC is paying 4% higher margin than Trepsico to Future group and other retailers. Ringo to giving Trepsico a run for its money. Trito's share has already been reduced considerably. Retail tieups, regional flavours, regional humour appeals have helped PTC. But PTC still wants a bigger share in the market and in foreign markets also, if possible.

## SWOT Analysis

**Question:** What is SWOT Analysis?

**Answer:** SWOT Analysis is a to used by organization for revolving strategic options For the future. The term SWOT refers to the analysis of strength, weaknesses, opportunities and threats facing a company. Strength and weaknesses are identify in the internal environment, whereas opportunities and threats are located in the external environment. Strength: Strength is an inherent capability of the organization which it can used to gain strategic advantage over its competitor. Weakness: A weakness is an inherent limitation or constraint of the organization which creates strategic disadvantage to it. Opportunity: An opportunity is a favourable condition in the external environment which enables to the organization its position. Threat: An unfavourable condition in external environment which cases a risk for, or damage to the organization position.

## Strengths of PTC

**Question:** What are the strength of PTC?

**Answer: The strength of PTC are: (a)** PTC has an existing distribution network that is used to its advantage; (b) the company has strengths in the area of procurement of potato, raw material to make the wafers; (c) financially the company is very strong as they are spending Rps.50 crores on advertising in a market wroth Rps. 250 crores; (d) the company has diverse flavous of welfares in its portfolio that are according to the different tastes of the target group; (e) PTC has done good bargaining deals with food bazaars and food chains; and (f) the cross-functional team of PTC made a virtuous marketing research.

## Weaknesses of PTC

**Question:** What are the weaknesses of PTC for entering into the branded snacks market?

**Answer:** Weaknesses are inherent limiting factors of an organization. They are internal by nature to the working of the organization. The case study does not clearly mention the points that can conclusively be weaknesses of the company. However, a deeper analysis will bring out that the company is totally new to the snacks business and is highly aggressive in its approach. The experience in the food business may not result in the required competencies in the business of chips. Seemingly, the company has also gone overboard in its advertisement expenditure. It may be that the margins justify expenditure of 20% in value of the total market size of Rps.250 Crores. Otherwise, the company may come into financial difficulties. Creating market may also be difficult as already there are many players who are trying to get attention of existing and new customers. The business is already clutered with regional and national players and is highly competitive. Further, the company is overly relying on young segment of the population. This segment can be highly receptive to the new products and the company may lose them easily to the competitors.

### Formulatation And Implementation Of Marketing Strategy For Ringo

**Question:** What kind of marketing strategy was formulated and implemented for Ringo? What else need to be done by Ringo so as to enlarge its market?

**Answer:** Formulation and implementation of marketing strategy was as: (a) the Product: To launch its snack product, an easy to remember brand name RINGO was decided upon, and to understand the snacking habits of Indian customer a large survey was undertaken, and also chefs on the basis of the market survey came out with sixteen flavours, and the target group was identified as youngsters of 15-24 years; (b) the Promotion: the Company spent about Rps.50 crore on marketing communication and different Media including print, electronic and outdoor advertising were put to use togetherwith an appeal used was that of humour, and a huge visibility through point-of-sale was also arranged and promotion policy was very aggressive considering that Rps.50 crores were spent in a market of Rps. 250 crores; the Place: getting Trito replaced by Ringo in Big-Bazaar and food bazaar chain of stores was a great success for PTC and to motivate a higher margin than the Trepsico was provided for.

PTC even otherwise has extensive distribution network. A perfect blend of marketing mix has made it possible to go so far and so early. Since the marketing strategy has remained successful, they need to carry it forward. However, they also need to keep a restrain on promotion as spending huge amount of money on marketing for a share in the market of Rps. 250 crores seems to be too high. Such an expensive campaign is only suitable if the company is able to increase the market size itself and not merely its own in the existing market share. To achieve this it requires competencies. Otherwise, it might be difficult to sustain high expenditure over a very long period of time.

## CASE STUDY 5:

Birsa Mining Ltd. (BML), has said in its mission statement that it will endeavour to make the maximum possible profit for its shareholders, whilst recognising its wider responsibility to society. BML has an opportunity to mine for gold at Nilachal Plateau, a remote and sparsely populated area. The mining process proposed, in this instance, means that all vegetation will be removed from the land concerned; after mining has finished, there will remain substantial lagoons full of poisonous water for at least a century. This mining process is a profitable one given the current price of gold. However, if the company were to reinstate the mined land, the process would be extremely unprofitable. The company has received permission from the Government to carry out the mining. The few local residents are opposed to the mining.

In view of the above – the readers should discuss the extent to which BML's mission statement is contradictory: (a) discuss how BML could establish a procedure whereby its wider responsibilities to society could be routinely considered when making strategic decisions; (b) advise BML how it could deal with strategies that present a conflict of objectives; and discuss the ethical dimensions of the decision to mine for gold.

## CASE STUDY 6:

AO Swift (Pvt.) Ltd was promoted nineteen years back as company manufacturing automobile parts with an investment of Rupees 5 crores by Abhishek Oberai. He took over as its chief executive and is occupying the same position till date. Abhishek an automobile engineer himself possessed rich experience of working abroad and in Hindustan Motors Ltd in India. He is dynamic and ready to take risk. He always emphasized on maintaining high quality standards. Initially, the products were supplied to automobile service centers all across the country. The market was small and the company suffered some losses.

Eight years after its inception the company entered into an agreement with Maruti Udyog Ltd to manufacture and supply specific components for their small car. This agreement was a turning point for the company. Later the company was able to enter agreements with other companies entering India. The company is able to manage a growth rate of over 25% in last five years. Its turnover in the last financial year exceeded 800 crores. The overall market is also witnessing a very high growth rate. Abhishek also possessed strong behavioural skills and allowed some autonomy and discretion to the senior managers of the company. A year back in an internal meeting Abhishek felt that the company can grow still faster if it enters other markets outside India.

Various options were analysed and efforts were made to discuss and negotiate with major manufacturers of the world. Getting some response from two manufacturers in European Union the company opened an office in London. Abhishek closely monitored the day-to-day working of this office. Having strategic implications all major decisions were taken by himself. He will also visit London every month to have first hand information about its working. However, as the company is growing it is becoming increasing difficult for him to manage this office. He also wants to expand further. He called a meeting with heads of various departments. In the meeting following alternatives were considered for foreign market: (a) continue to manufacture products in India and export them to other countries; (b) initiate manufacturing activities in other countries; and (c) takeover existing manufacturers of the products.

### Reasons for AO Awift Ltd to Open Office in London

**Question:** Write a note on reasons for AO Swift Ltd to open office in London?

**Answer:** The readers should answer this question as an exercise and practice.

### Strategy in a High Growth Market

**Question:** What should be the strategy of the company in a high growth market and why?

**Answer:** The readers should answer this question as an exercise and practice.

### Analysis of Alternatives

## Role of Strategic Management in Business Organizations

**Question:** Make an analysis of various alternatives that are being considered for expanding in foreign markets?

**Answer:** The readers should answer this question as an exercise and practice.

### CASE STUDY 7:

Chemical Ltd, a quoted chemical company, has until recently achieved a steady increase in profitability over a number of years. It faces stern competition and the directors are concerned about the dissatisfaction expressed by major shareholders regarding performance over the last two years. During this period, it has consistently increased dividends, but its share price has not grown at the same rate as it did previously Khemco Ltd, a direct competitor, is similarly experiencing a reduction in profitability. Its shareholders are diverse, with the majority being financial institutions. Khemco Ltd. has been criticised for under-investment and has achieved no product development over the last-two years. Following a concerted media campaign, Khemco Ltd. is facing prosecution for discharging untreated pollutants into a river. Chemical Ltd. is seriously considering making a bid to acquire Khemco Ltd. The directors of Chemicals Ltd, however, are divided as to whether Khemco should be closed down or permitted to continue production post-acquisition, if a bid is made. In either situation significant staff redundancies would follow.

In the light of the above – the readers should discuss the following questions:

> ➢ State the strategic factors which Chemicals would need to consider before making a bid to acquire Khemco Ltd.
> ➢ (a) discuss the social and ethical implications for the managers and staff of both the companies, if the acquisition goes ahead; and (b) discuss the environmental issues which would face the directors of Chemicals Ltd if it proceeds with the acquisition of Khemco Ltd.

## CASE STUDY 8:

Sweet Drinks Ltd is a drinks company whose core business is manufacturing and selling soft drinks to 80,000 outlets throughout India. The business of the company is good with annual turnover exceeding three billon of rupees. Profits are good and shareholders are often rewarded with lucrative dividends and bonuses. Four years back the company has diversified into the alcoholic drinks industry and has taken-over two small breweries located in western India. The company has also diversified into hotels with purchase of twenty-five hotels of three/four star category across the country. To its advantage the company has been able to obtain a monopoly for the sale of its soft drinks in its hotels and is beginning to establish itself as a brand name in the brewery industry.

Part of the strategy of the company is to continue to purchase hotels, particular by targeting National Capital Region of Delhi where tourism is likely to pick up with the forthcoming Commonwealth Games. The company also intends to construct a five star hotel in Gurgoan to take tax advantage announced recently by the finance ministers. Everything was going on well until recently, when a Public Interest Litigation from NGO accused the company of indulging in surrogate advertising of its brewery products. In fact the company has similar brand names for its soft drinks and brewery products. This triggered a lot of protests and demonstrations against the company. Newspapers were flooded with the articles against the company. There were also some demonstrations and some small incidents of stone pelting in a few of its hotels.

The readers should answer the following questions as a practice exercise.

➤ Discuss the factors related to SWOT analyses for the company?
➤ Explain how Sweet Drinks Ltd is achieving synergy?
➤ Explain the nature of diversification adopted by the company?

## CASE STUDY 9:

You have recently been appointed to head the management accounting department of A (P) Ltd (APL), which is a small engineering company engaged in the manufacture of precision parts. The market in which the company sells its products is small and APL faces severe competition. Dun to the production facilities available, the company is able to undertake only small-scale engineering work. Large scale engineering jobs are turned away as the company does not possess the manufacturing facilities to undertake them. At best, it can act only as agent for another contractor to do the work.

The board of APL is aware that the volume of work which is being turned away is increasing. This is particularly frustrating as the company is unable to utilise its capacity to the fullest extent all the time. APL has achieved a steady increase in profit over the last few years. Nevertheless, the board of the company believes that it could increase profitability still further by expanding and thus being able to carry out the larger scale work which is currently being turned away. Budgetary control and standard costing information has, for many years, been provided as the sole output of the management accounting department. The previous management accountant prided himself on the punctuality and comprehensiveness of the reports produced. Each job is priced by adding a percentage of its total cost calculated in accordance with the company's standard costing procedures.

The annual cost budget is split into monthly parts and flexed to take account of a particular period's actual production. Monthly cost variances, comprising those for direct materials, direct labour, variable and fixed production overheads, are produced and provided to the relevant managers. In addition, sales price and volume variances are produced by the management accounting department each period. The company does not have a marketing department although new customers are obtained from advertising within professional engineering journals and by attendance at trade shows.

At one such trade show, the managing director was introduced to the concept of benchmarking. He believes that there may be advantages in APL undertaking benchmarking.

In the light of the above – the readers should discuss the following:

➢ In consideration of the need for the board of APL to be provided with information which assists its strategic decision making, comment critically on the management accounting reports, currently provided.
➢ State and justify what changes you, as management accountant, would make in

providing information which facilitates strategic planning in the company. (Within your answer, describe what financial and non-financial information you would supply which is different from that, already provided).

➤ Explain the concept of benchmarking and suggest how it might be applied to information for strategicplanning in APL.

## CASE STUDY 10:

A transport company was engaged in handling cargo between selected inter-city routes and had a fleet of trucks numbering ten. After recent elections to the State Assembly, the Chief Minister of the State announced infrastructure development to be taken up as the top priority by the State Government. Bids were invited for road construction on a large scale. Work started within six months. Accordingly, the transport company decided to expand its operations adding on more trucks to its fleet. Meanwhile, industrial growth rate in the State had a setback due to labour unrest which seriously hampered production in several industries. The transport company found its operations unprofitable.

In the light of the above – the readers should answer the following:

➤ What was the flaw in the planning for expanded operations?
➤ Is there any remedy to the situation?

**CASE STUDY 11:**

Laboni Stores Ltd, for more than ten years till 1995, was successfully running a number of retail stores selling cosmetics and skin care products. From 1996, sales were stagnating and now after a year had started declining. The general manager of the company made enquiries from stores in charge at various location of stores. All of them reported that ladies, particularly the younger generation, were found to be highly discriminating about choice of products. Demand for certain branded items widely fluctuated due to movie artists' preferences shown on the TV. Also there is a marked tendency to equate quality with rice. The general manager decided to have environmental analysis carried out with a focus on changes in social and cultural factors among urban ladies. On that basis he even thought of recommending to the Board of Directors a complete change in the product lines to be decided.

In the light of the above – the readers should answer the following questions:

➢ Do you think the GM was right in his approach regarding environmental scanning?
➢ What other factors in the environment needed analysis? If there was a clear change in the tastes and preferences of buyers of certain products, is it essential for the company to switch over to a different product line?

**CASE STUDY 12:**

Viking Sewing Machines Ltd., a large company, was engaged in manufacturing and marketing household sewing machines including electronic models and low-priced mechanical models. Sale of domestic sewing machines was declining all over the world in view of the increasing popularity of ready-made garments produced by companies using industrial sewing machines. At this stage there was a change in the ownership of Viking in 1997, when the CEO resigned and a new CEO took charge. Under his leadership, Viking considered the following mission statements for the company: (a) to develop, produce, market and sell sewing machines and related products which enhance the joy of creative sewing; (b) to be a consumer-driven company ensuring growth, profitability and success by providing superior satisfaction to the consumers and our dealer partners by continuously adding value to the Viking Brand; (c) to be recognised as the leading premier sewing machine company in the world; and (d) to expand our business by creating demand for more creative uses of sewing.

In the light of the above – the readers should answer the following question:

➢ Which one of the above mission statements should the company adopt and why?

## CASE STUDY 13:

Samuel Enterprises had started producing and selling liquor in 1980 and gradually expanded its business to include manufacture of chemicals for pharma companies as well as construction work. With three different divisions, there was a clear change noticeable after 1991 in their sales performance profitability. Earlier, 60 p.c. of sales revenue was from liquor business, while the share of other two divisions was about 20 p.c. each. While the market for liquor was gradually shrinking due to prohibition in many areas, sales of chemicals had an uncertain potential due to the expansion of Indian producers and entry of multinational companies and introduction of new technology.

The construction industry on the other hand had a high growth potential due to emphasis on infrastructure development as a part of government economic policy. The company wanted to hive off one of the divisions and focus on developing of the other two divisions. The Managing Director was in favour of undertaking an exercise in portfolio analysis for a strategic decision. However, some non-executive directors were of opinion that analysis of division-wise capabilities was also necessary besides using any portfolio matrix model before arriving at a strategic decision.

In the light of the above – the readers should discuss the following:

> Comment on the suggestions of MD and other directors giving reasons for against their respective views.

**CASE STUDY 14:**

A transport company with nation-wide operations is now experiencing a difficult time with uneconomic freight rates and severe competition. It has diversified its business setting up textile mills and a wire rod mill in Karnataka. All these units have been hit by severe power cuts imposed in the State. Still the company is considering several expansion strategies since the transport operations are expected to revive in the near future.

In the light of the above – the readers should discuss the following:

➤ What should be the appropriate strategy of the company?
➤ Give reasons!

### CASE STUDY 15:

A well-known company engaged in manufacturing metal containers and packaging had diversified its operations in early 1980s investing a huge amount in a bearings factory. After 8 years, the company was suffering from a high cost structure, mounting losses, shortage of liquid funds and large scale exodus of technicians and managers. Management's proposal for reduction in workforce and wage cuts is not acceptable to labour unions with the result that 3 of its packaging units had to be shut down. The factories need to be opened immediately for revival of business which depends upon cost reduction through reduction in the excess workforce.

In the light of the above – the readers should discuss the following:

➤ Suggest, with proper justification, a suitable turnaround strategy for the company.

### CASE STUDY 16:

A company manufacturing certain well-known brands of malted food, chocolates and biscuits for more than a decade ventured into manufacture of apple juice in 1981, but had to sell off the plant in 1984. During the year 1987, the company's sales were higher by 19 p.c. over the previous year despite new competition. Production of chocolates increased by 14 p.c. and of malted food by 22 p.c. The sale of biscuits was also higher although these were processed by third parties and sold under popular brand names of the company. Having satisfactory financial results in 1987, the company decided to diversify into computer software business.

In the light of the above – the readers should answer the following questions:

- ➤ Was it the right strategic decision?
- ➤ What could be the possible reasons underlying the company's decision to diversify into software business?

## CASE STUDY 17:

A company manufacturing small electric appliances (irons, toasters and mixers) is planning to add room airconditioners to its product line by buying out another firm. Made in a separate plant in a different city the air--conditioners would be sold by a sales force under a different brand name to the same customers-retail chain stores, large departmental stores, and hardware and appliance wholesalers.

In the light of the above – the readers should answe the following questions:

- ➤ Does this seem to be a wise addition to the product line?
- ➤ Why or why not? Explain. How will the central marketing managers be affected by it?

## CASE STUDY 18:

The Chief Executive of a company manufacturing light engineering goods (pump sets and 2 H.P. motors)

stated, "Our wage rates should continue to be among
the highest in the country. Our competitors will have to
match any increase we given and the higher wage cost
can be passed on to the customers." The finance
manager of a competing enterprise observed, "We have
a social responsibility to check the wage-price spiral.
Our men are already well paid and further increase will
only add fuel to inflation."

In the light of the above – the readers should
answer the following questions:

➢ Which of the above wage policies is more
reasonable and pragmatic?
➢ Under what conditions can a company be able to
pass on wage increases to its customers through
a price rise?
➢ What importance, if any, should a company
attach to the inflationary effect of its wage policy?

## CASE STUDY 19:

After ten years of struggle, a company
manufacturing radio sets and computers, surfaced in
1982-83 to make a profit of Rps. 641akhs and then Rps.
1.14 crores in 1983-84, but again slipped back to Rps.
1.10 crore loss in the accounting period that followed. It
is reported that the company's radio division was
unlikely ever to pay its way, its computers failed to
make a splash, and its earlier efforts to diversify were
yet to bear fruit.

According to a high-level executive, the company
concentrated on manufacturing when it needed a
marketing orientation. When a new CEO was appointed,
his remedy for revival was to divisionalise the

organisation, introduce more accountability and diversify into cable TV and other areas.

In the light of the above – the readers should answer the following questions:

> What could possibly have gone wrong with the implementation of the company's strategy?
> Comment on the measures of revival suggested by the new CEO!

## CASE STUDY 20:

Fifty years ago, the typical automobile manufacturing companies purchased most of their parts from other manufacturers. They did little more than assemble the parts into complete automobiles. Currently many manufacturers of automobiles, large ones mainly, manufacture 75 to 80 p.c. of the parts that go into a typical automobile.

In the light of the above – the readers should reply the following:

> Give possible reasons underlying this shift towards more integrated production.

## CASE STUDY 21:

Avik Industries Ltd. was a family-owned conglomerate with diversified business activities including consumers durables, switchgears, batteries, and both toilet and washing soaps. For a number of years the company prospered with growth in volumes and market share. But its performance had setback in 1999, when the net margins in switchgears, the most profitable product, declined from 12 to 11%, while in consumer durables it had halved to 6%, the batteries business was under pressure, and the ailing soaps division had just started looking up. The Chief Executive of the switchgear unit observed that the results would have been worse but for the focus on operational efficiency. For years, Avik had been organised along four divisions as independent profit centres. Except for HR and finance, all other functions were decentralised. The advantage was that each of the businesses had a strong focus. It also facilitated customer focus.

The flipside was that divisions became insular and inward-looking. Each division had its own ad budget-even separate ad agencies. The sales force was pushed to look at short-term product promotions in the face of competitive pressure. The cost of sales was rising much faster than rate of growth in sales. It seemed divisional autonomy had been pushed too far down the line.

In the light of the above – the readers should answer the following questions:

 ➢ Should the divisional set-up be disbanded?
 ➢ Or, should the divisions be converted into SBUs and spun off into separate companies? Is there any other alternative structure possible?

## CASE STUDY 22:

Nath Ltd is a small family controlled manufacturing company of Howrah. In its around 60-year history, the company has grown to the extent that it now employs 75 staff, producing a wide and diverse range of industrial products and special components: The company has increased in size from its small original base. However, it has never employed a strategic management approach for its development and has relied on operational decision-making to determine priorities. Nath Ltd. has never gathered any information relating to its markets. In recent years, the company has experienced a reduction. in turnover and profitability and is assessing how it might redress -the situation.

In the light of the above – the readers should discuss the following:

> You explain how strategic management differs from operational management to your father and uncles, the directors of Nath Ltd. After being convinced, the directors of Nath Ltd. have now decided to introduce a strategic management approach which will assist in the selection of appropriate strategies for future development of the company.
> Discuss the cultural and organisational changes which Nath Ltd. will need to implement in order to successfully introduce strategic management.

## CASE STUDY 23:

Agrico Ltd. was in chemical, fertiliser and pesticide business since 1998. The company had reasonable earnings till 2002. For the next 3 years, sales in all the divisions went on declining and by 2005, the company was in the red. The Managing Director was thinking of internal benchmarking as a possible way out. A senior executive suggested that functional benchmarking would be more appropriate. The Finance Manager was of the view that the problem was that of economic recession in the relevant product lines. The M.D. was unable to decide on the matter.

In the light of the above – the readers should discuss the following:

➢ Suggest the most suitable benchmarking for Agrico Ltd. with justification.

## CASE STUDY 24:

In 1997, a leading manufacturer of personal computer took the decision to set up its Indian manufacturing base near Bangalore. Its decision was seen as a success for the Karnataka Development Corporation, which had been hoping since 1993 to attract the computer manufacturer to Karnataka.

In the light of the above – the readers should discuss the following:

➢ What do you think would be the objectives of the Karnataka Development Corporation (KDC) and how might its objectives and those of the computer manufacturer be expected to coincide in the matter of choosing a location for the Indian manufacturing base?
➢ Describe the environmental factors which you think might have been influential in making the computer manufacturer decide to locate its operation near Bangalore in Karnataka, and how the KDC might have tried to exploit these influences.

## CASE STUDY 25:

Nirjas Ltd is engaged in the production of floral concentrates which have uses in a wide variety of fields, from cosmetics to toiletries. At the moment the concentrates are produced and sold to perfume manufacturers, who in turn supply the producers of the ultimate products. The directors of Nirjas are concerned about the higher profitability at the product end of the trade compared with the production of the concentrates, and ask you to explore the possibilities of vertical expansion.

In the light of the above – the readers should answer the following:

➢ What are the main issues to be examined?

# Chapter 9

## SUMMARY AND CONCLUSION

Strategic management is the process by which the business strategy formulated is put into action. It includes the design and management of organizational systems to achieve the best integration of people and structure, allocating resources, managing human resources and developing information and decision processes to achieve organizational objectives. Pierce and Robinson noted that "to effectively direct and control the use of the firm's resources, mechanisms such as organizational structure, information systems, leadership styles, assignment of key managers, budgeting, rewards, and control systems are essential strategy implementation ingredients"[38].

After the creative and analytical aspects of the corporate strategy have been formulated the priority of the management is to convert the strategy into operationally effective action. A strategy is never complete, until it gains a commitment of the firm's resources and becomes embodied in its organizational structure. Strategy implementation is an iterative process of implementing strategies, policies, programs and action plans that allows a firm to utilize its resources to take advantage of opportunities in the competitive environment. It can also be defined: "strategy implementation as an iterative, dynamic and a complex process, which comprises of series of decisions

---

[38] Strategic Management: Formulation, Implemen... and Control by John Pearce and Richard Robinson (Aug 2002)

and activities by the management and the administration those affected by many interrelated internal and external factors, to turn strategic plans into reality in order to achieve the objectives of the firm."

If strategy is to achieve organizational goals, it is imperative that implementation and controls are firmly in place within the hierarchy of the organizational system and also strategy is implemented through the effective use of four main management functions, namely: planning, organizing, leading, and controlling. The planning function should involve effective integration and coordination of activities to ensure that implementation is on schedule and also follows the right direction.

The organizing function should involve wise allocation of human resources by defining tasks and assigning responsibilities to individuals as well as groups. The leading function should provide effective leadership for the organization, communicating stately, and motivating the employees to achieve the best results.

The controlling function should involve controlling resources, tracking results and providing feedback for making any needed adjustments to the strategy. However, rise of knowledge and technology, in this electronic age, has dramatic implications on the traditional organizations, thereby making it more complex to develop a long-term strategy based on knowledge and technology that could soon be obsolete.

Personal computers, fax machines, cell phones, and internet (i.e. new interactive technologies) have compressed the amount of time it takes to get information, make decision and take action and consequently have reset the clock on real time. In strategic management it has become necessary to respond to changing circumstances and customer expectations in the smallest possible lapse of time. Therefore, it is vital to build speed in our strategic thinking and implement this strategy at all levels of the organization.

We may conclude this discussion by making an analogy between a physician and a strategist. They both look at the symptoms and make the most probable diagnosis and prescribe the best medicine (or procedure) to cure the illness. If prescription (strategic implementation) does not work, they may believe that they have made a wrong diagnosis (strategic choice), and then they may make another diagnosis. This implies that since physicians do not give up, if first diagnosis does not work, strategists also should not give up and make another strategic choice.

# BIBLIOGRAPGY

1. Abell, D.F.: *Defining the Business*: The Starting Point of Strategic Planning (Englewood Cliffs, N.J.: Prentice-Hall, 1980).
2. Alexander, L.D. (1985), "Successfully Implementing Strategic Decisions". *Long Range Planning*, 18, 91-97.
3. Allio, M.K. (2005), "A Short, Practical Guide to Implementing Strategy". *Journal of Business Strategy*, 26, 12-21.
4. Ansoff, H. I.: *Implementing Strategic Management* (Englewood Cliffs, N.J.: Prentice-Hall, 1985).
5. Ansoff, H.I.: "Strategy Formulation as a Learning Process: An Applied Managerial Theory of Strategic Behavior, "*International Studies of Management & Organization*, vol.7 (Summer 1977),pp.58-77.
6. Bazzaz, S. J., and P. H. Grinyer: "Corporate Planning in the U.K.: The State of the art in the 70s," *Strategic Management Journal,* vol. 2 (April-June, 1981), pp. 155-168.
7. Boswell, J.S.: *Business Policies in the Making* (London: George, Allen & Unwin, 1983).
8. Chaffee, E.E.: "Three Models of Strategy," Academy of Management Review, vol. 10(1985), pp.89-98.
9. Curtis, D.A (ed.): *Strategic Planning for Smaller Business* (Boston: Heath, 1983).
10. Floyd, S.W., and Wooldridge, B. (1992a). „Managing Strategic Consensus: The Foundation of Effective Implementation". *Academy of Management Executive,* 6, 27-39.
11. Floyd, S.W., and Wooldridge, B. (1992b). „Middle Management Involvement in Strategy and Its Association with Strategic Type: A Research Note". *Strategic Management Journal,* 13, 153-167.
12. Floyd, S.W., and Wooldridge, B. (1997). „Middle Managements Strategic Influence and Organizational Performance". *Journal of Management Studies, 34,* 465-485.
13. Ginter, P.M., and D. D. White: "Asocial Learning Approach to Strategic Management: Toward a Theoretical Foundation," Academy of Management Review, vol. 7 (1982). pp. 253-261.

14. Gotcher, J. W.: "Strategic Planning in European Multinationals," *Long Range Planning* (October, 1977), pp. 7-13.
15. Govindarajan, V. (1988), :A Contingency Approach to Strategy Implementation at the Business-Unit Level Integrating Administrative Mechanisms With Strategy". *Academy of Management Journal,* 31, 828-853.
16. Govindarajan, V. (1989), "Implementing Competitive Strategies at the Business Unit Level: Implications of Matching Managers to Strategies". *Strategic Management Journal*, 10, 251-269.
17. Govindarajan,V., and Fisher.J. (1990), "Strategy, Control systems, and resource sharing: effects on business-Unit Performance". *Academy of Management Journal,* 33, 259-285.
18. Gupta, A.K., and Govindarajan, V. (1984). „Business Unit Strategy, Managerial Characteristics and Business Unit Effectiveness at Strategy Implementation". *Academy of Management Journal,* 27, 25-41.
19. Hall, W.K.: "SBUs: Hot, New Topic in the management of Diversification," Business Horizons, vol. 21 (February 1978), pp. 17-25.
20. Hatten, M. L., "Strategic Management in Not-for-Profit Organizations," *Strategic Management Journal*, vol. 3(1982), pp.89-104.
21. Hay, R.D.: *Strategic Management for Non-Profit Organizations* (Santa Barbara, Calif.: Kinko's 1986).
22.    Heide, M., Grønhaug, K.,and Johannessen, S. (2002). „Exploring Barriers to The Successful Implementation of a Formulated strategy". Scandinavian Journal of Management, 18, 217-231.
23. Henry, H. W.: "Then and Now: A Look at Strategic Planning Systems," *Journal of Business Strategy*, vol. 1 (Winter 1981), pp. 64-69.
24. Heracleous, L. 2003. *Strategy and Organization: Realizing Strategic Management.* Cambridge: Cambridge University Press.
25. Heracleous, L. 2006. *Discourse, Interpretation, Organization.* Cambridge: Cambridge University Press.

26. Heracleous, L., Wirtz, J., and Pangarkar, N. 2009. *Flying High in a Competitive Industry: Secrets of the World's Leading Airline*. McGraw-Hill.
27. Heracleous, L. & Jacobs, C. 2011. *Crafting Strategy: Embodied Metaphors in Practice*. Cambridge: Cambridge University Press.
28. Hrebiniak, L.G. (2006), "Obstacles to Effective Strategy Implementation". *Organizational Dynamics*, 35, 12-31
29. Hrebiniak, Lawrence G. and Snow, Charles C., "Decision-making-in-management; Organizational-effectiveness". *Human Relation (HR), 35, 1139-57*
30. Hobbs, J.M., and DR Heany: "Coupling Strategy to Operating Plans*," Harvard Business Review*, vol. 55(May-June 1977), pp. 119-126.
31. Hyashi. K. : "Corporate Planning Practices in Japanese Multinationals, " *Academy of Management Journa*l, vol. 21 (1978), pp. 211-226.
32. Dr Khan, Wazir Ali, 'Applied Management for Engineers and technologists' ISBN 0-9526436-2-6
33. Dr Khan, Wazir Ali, 'Professional Manual on Total Quality Management' - ISBN 0-9526436-1-8
34. Dr Khan, Wazir Ali, 'Professional Manual on Total Project Management (Volume 1: CM General Perspective)'- ISBN 0-9526436-3-4
35. Dr Khan, Wazir Ali, 'Professional Manual on Total Project Management' (Volume 2: CM Commercial Perspective)'- ISBN 0-9526436-4-2
36. Dr Khan, Wazir Ali, 'Professional Manual on Claims Management and Dispute Resolution in Construction Process' - 0-9526436-7-7
37. Dr Khan, Wazir Ali, 'Fundamentals of Human Resources Development (First Edition)' - ISBN 0-9526436-0-X
38. Kim, W.C., and Mauborgne, R.A. (1993). „Making Global Strategies Work". *Sloan Management Review*, 34, 11-27.
39. Kudla, R.J.: "Elements of Effective Corporate Planning," *Long Range Planning, vol.* 9, no. 4 (August 1976), pp. 82-93.
40. Lachman, R.: "public and Private Sector Differences," *Academy of Management Journal*, vol. 28 (1985), pp. 671-680.

# Role of Strategic Management in Business Organizations

41. Lehner, J. (2004). „Strategy Implementation Tactics as Response to Organizational, Strategic, and Environmental Imperatives". *Management Revue*, 15, 460-480
42. Miller, D.: "Common Syndromes of Business Failure, "*Business Horizons*, vol. 20(November 1977), pp. 43-53.
43. Noble, C.H. (1999a, "Building the Strategy Implementation Network". *Business Horizons*, 19-27.
44. Noble,C.H. (1999b). "The Eclectic Roots of Strategy Implementation Research". *Journal of Business Research,* 45, 119-134.
45. Noble, C.H., and Mokwa, M.P. (1999). „Implementing Marketing Strategies: Developing and Testing a Managerial Theory". *Journal of Marketing,* 63, 57-73.
46. Nutt, P.C.: "A Strategic Planning Network for Non-profit Organizations," *Strategic Management Journal*, vol.5 (1984), pp.57-75.
47. Nutt, P.C. (1986), "Tactics of Implementation". *Academy of Management Journal*. 29, 230-261.
48. Pangarkar, N., Singh, K. and Heracleous, L. 2010. *Business Strategy in Asia: A Casebook (3rd ed)*. Cengage.
49. Peng, W., and Litteljohn, D. (2001), "Organisational Communication and Strategy Implementation-A Primary Inquiry". *International Journal of Contemporary Hospitality*, 13, 360-363.
50. Porter, M. E.: Competitive Strategy (New York: Free Press, 1985).
51. Rapert, M.I., Lynch, D., and Suter, T. (1996), "Enhancing Functional and Organizational Performance via Strategic Consensus and Commitment". *Journal of Strategic Marketing*, 4, 193-205.
52. Rapert, M.I., Velliquette, A., and Garretson, J.A. (2002). „The Strategic Implementation Process Evoking Strategic Consensus through Communication". *Journal of Business Research*, 55, 301-310.
53. Rapert, Molly Inhofe and Brent Wren (1998), "Reconsidering Organizational Structure: A Dual Perspective of Frameworks

54. Ring, P.S. and J. L. Perry: "Strategic Management in Public and Private Organizations," *Academy of Management Review*, vol. 10 (1985), pp. 276-286.
55. Shirley, R.C., "Limiting the Scope of Strategy: A Decision Based Approach," Academy of Management Review, vol. 7 (1982). pp. 262-268.
56. Slater, S.F., and Olson, E.M. (2001), "Marketing"s Contribution to the Implementation of Business Strategy: An Empirical Analysis". *Strategic Management Journal*. 22, 1055-1067
57. Vancil, R.F.: "Strategy Formulation in Complex Organizations," *Sloan Management Review,* vol. 17 (Winter 1976), pp. 1-18.
58. Walker, Jr, O.C., and Ruekert, R.W. (1987), "Marketing"s Role in The Implementation of Business Strategies: A Critical Review and Conceptual Framework". *Journal of Marketing,* 51, 15-33.

www.ingramcontent.com/pod-product-compliance
Lightning Source LLC
Chambersburg PA
CBHW071306220526
45468CB00001B/284